FUNDAMENTAL ACTIVITIES

OURSELVES · OUR WORLD · OUR INSTRUMENTS

Production Team

Kate Baxter
Sarah Knight
Lis McCullough
Bridget McLeod
Wendy Reynolds
Jenny Tilley

Thanks and acknowledgements

Sincere thanks to:

All those who took part in making the video-cassette; they are mentioned individually on the credit-roll

Authors and illustrator of video notes: Bridget McLeod, Wendy Reynolds, Hannah Cockerill

Video duplicating co-ordinator: Simon Peck (Nottingham Audio Visual Services Ltd)

Presentation pack designer: Peter Salisbury (Edward Markall Ltd)

Marketing co-ordinator: Malcolm Pallant

Printing co-ordinator: Hugh Barnes (Barnes & Humby Ltd)

Photographs for montage: Chris Shaw

Text preparation: Heather Savage, Jo Swain, Jenny Tilley

Text readers: Frances Grene, Lis McCullough, Vanessa Owen, Doreen Tharby

Text processor: Ann Booth

Advisory consultant: Ray Johnson

Graphic artist: Sarah Knight

Editorial Adviser: John Bowkett

The Production Team pay tribute to the inspiration they have received from the teachings of the following Music Educators: Jaques Dalcroze, Zoltan Kodaly, Rudolf Laban, Carl Orff, John Paynter, Murray Schafer

Acknowledgement: Thomas Nelson & Sons Ltd for permission to include "You Can't See" from a book of Music Games "Pompaleerie Jig"

Every effort has been made to trace and acknowledge copyright owners. If any right has been omitted this will be rectified in subsequent editions following notification.

Published by Fundamental Activities, PO Box 149, Nottingham NG3 5PU

© 1994 Kate Baxter

ISBN 0 9523043 0 9

Printed in Great Britain by Barnes & Humby Ltd, Nottingham

CONTENTS

INTRODUCING FUNDAMENTAL ACTIVITIES

Fundamental Activities is planned as a long-term resource, so there are a lot of activities in the sixty-six pages of the handbook. The video and the notes that go with it offer you a chance to see some of the ideas in action. The handbook tells you more about what you see on the video and describes other activities, to enable you to explore new pathways. You can use the suggestions we give, either as self-contained activities, or as part of your own ongoing programme of music-making.

Pick an idea that appeals to you and give it a try. As you actually use the activities and start to get feedback from the group or individual you are working with, you will build up the confidence to adapt the ideas to your particular needs, and to develop them. Through adaptation and development you will make the ideas your own with unique touches that suit your style and situation.

Finally, we hope you won't forget the fun that we believe should always be part of Fundamental Activities. If the fun's there, together with conviction and a sense of purpose, then learning and personal development will follow.

INTRODUCING OURSELVES

Getting Started
When beginning a session the introduction time is crucial for breaking the ice and helping everyone to relax. Allow time for the creative process of sharing names, hearing voices and the giving and receiving of contributions. Be aware of those who do not want to be actively involved.

Open with a greeting routine – safely familiar or adventurously new. It could set the mood for the session.

A Meeting Greeting
Sing a personal hello to everyone in the room in turn
Hello John Wells, are you feeling good today?
Hello Maria . . . happy birthday
Hello my friend with the smart new hair cut
Hello Lily, will you dance for us again today?
Extend ideas from any responses you may get
Spontaneity is fun for the whole group

Ready Wrap
Start a "boom-cha" pulse with body sounds
Leader: My name is Bert and I come from Brazil
Everyone: His name is Bert and he comes from Brazil
Leader: My friend's called Betty and she eats beans
Everyone: His friend's called Betty and she eats beans
Keep it cool . . . Keep it moving . . . but . . . Take it easy

The New You
Angela, if you were a colour what would you be?
Ben, if you were an animal what would you be?
Andrew, if you were a fabric what would you be?
Denise, if you were a musical instrument what would you be?
Pick up and develop from the answers

A Touching Hello
Take time to shake hands with everyone in the room
Did you greet everyone?
Start again but this time pretend to be . . .
Kings and Queens . . . regal or pompous
Spies . . . sinister and secretive
Aliens . . . hostile or inquisitive
Friends . . . it's up to you!

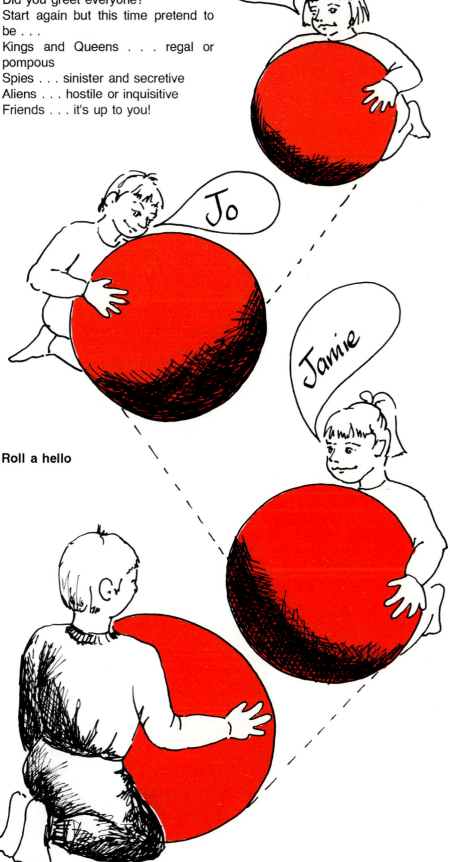

Roll a hello

1

WARM–UPS

(L)egg Mayonnaise

Sing to the tune of "Good King Wenceslas"

Up and down and up and down
Marching to the music
Lift those knees without a frown
You can really do it
Point that foot and bend it back
Point and back you bring it
Make a circle as you go
Round and round you swing it

Second time . . . other leg

Wakey–Shakey–Wakey

Wiggle your toes. Shake that foot. Now the other one. Add legs, hips and then the upper body. Gently mix in the head and shoulders, whisking down the arms to the fingers until you're shakin' all over. Allow to cool down slowly. Fold in a few deep breaths and you'll be ready for the next course!
Season to taste with assorted shakers.

Oil 'n' Vigour

Slowly circle your shoulders in turn. Imagine drops of oil lubricating and easing the joint. Extend the circle to include elbows and then arms, feeling the stretch in the upper arm. Enjoy the freedom of the movement as the whole of the upper part of the body becomes supple.

Spaghetti Stretch

Curl up as small as you can on the floor or in your chair. When the cymbal starts you are going to begin to uncurl gently. Think about how you are going to start. The cymbal starts to play quietly. As it gets louder gradually stretch up and up and up until your arms and fingers are fully extended. When the cymbal crashes breathe out and relax. Open your mouth. Let out a big yawn. Stretch those arms. Use finger massage on the skin as you work your mouth and jaw. Make chewing gum faces. Yawn again.

The message underlying these fun starters is that they are important. Relaxed bodies are more responsive due to the awakening of the nervous system.

OURSELVES: Body Percussion

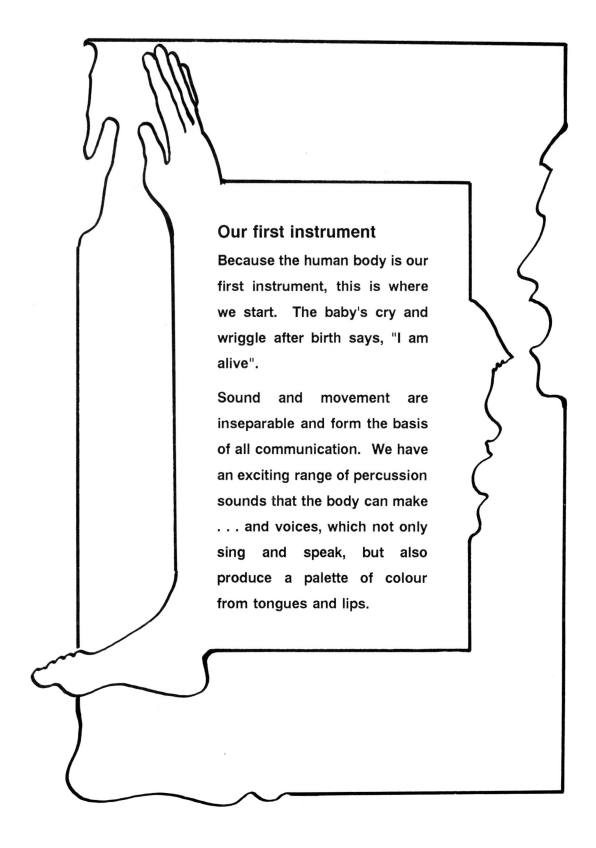

Our first instrument

Because the human body is our first instrument, this is where we start. The baby's cry and wriggle after birth says, "I am alive".

Sound and movement are inseparable and form the basis of all communication. We have an exciting range of percussion sounds that the body can make . . . and voices, which not only sing and speak, but also produce a palette of colour from tongues and lips.

OURSELVES: Body Percussion
Follow my Leader

An activity using body sounds
★Leader starts making body sounds and asks everyone to join in. Take time on each one until everybody's got it.

★This sequence starts with hands and finishes with feet – but mix your own, adding spicy speed changes and colouring variety.

★Heighten the listening and looking with a short pause ⌒ occasionally and sometimes play with a beat and sometimes without, eg teeth scraping
★Make a real FINISH with the STAMPS and a loud 'WHOOP' with hand wobbling over mouth
This is fun.

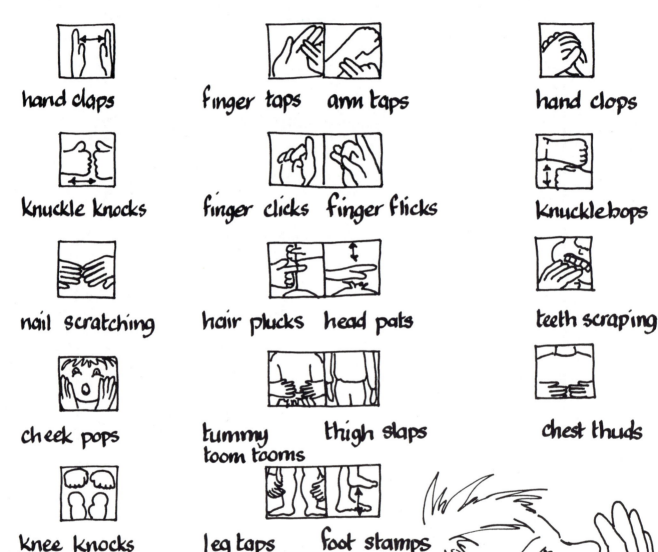

hand claps

finger taps   arm taps

hand claps

knuckle knocks

finger clicks   finger flicks

knuckle bops

nail scratching

hair plucks   head pats

teeth scraping

cheek pops

tummy toom tooms   thigh slaps

chest thuds

knee knocks

leg taps   foot stamps

Feeling safe in a joining–in activity encourages attentive looking, listening and concentration – the basis for all communication.

Let the group learn about the physical structure of the body and discover that clapping is only one of a wide range of body sounds.

Help them to focus on

★*personal awareness of their bodies.*
★*the sounds that they make and feeling OK about them*

The activity ends with a loud "WHOOP", taking the body sounds into the important area of the voice (page 23)

4

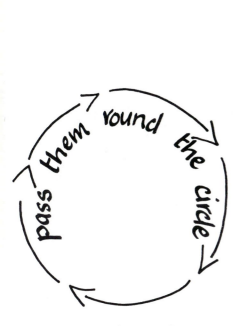

pass them round the circle

plishk *shrinkle* *shriggle* *Plak* *roggle*

Every body sound belongs to a 'family' of instruments . . .
Bones – Claves, Xylophones
Hollows – Drums
Hair and whiskers – Guitars, Harps
Mouth and voice – Flutes, Trumpets

Meet all the families on the following pages.
There is one family whose sounds the human body cannot make . . . unless . . . (p 50)

After exploring the sounds you can make

Pass them round a circle . . .

★Stand or sit in a circle
★Leader chooses a person to start . . . Frank
★Frank chooses one body sound, makes it and then "passes" the sound to the next person in the circle, Annie. Frank stops making his sound. Make a BIG feature of the way the sound is passed, emphasising the movement involved in passing a sound from one person to another.
★Annie passes her sound to the next person, and so on all the way round. Aim to try and keep the sound and movement as continuous as possible.

Find ways of combining and listening to 2, 3 or 4 sounds together.
Which work well together?
Which are your favourites?
Which could be used again?
Create your own descriptive words and make mobiles.

WOO WOO WOO WOO WOO

★When the sound arrives back to Frank again the Leader chooses another member of the group to start the whole thing off again. This could be done by gesture (passing the leadership across the circle), or contact (gentle pressure on the shoulders of another member of the group), or by name (calling or singing the name of the next starting person).

Fun Song
The wonderful thing about bodies
Is bodies make wonderful sounds
Your hands on your rump go bumpetty bump
What sounds can you make with your ---?

More exploration . . .
★You have 30 seconds to find as many sounds as you can using your hands, feet and all other parts of your body, first individually and then in pairs.

★Explore sounds that depend on two people . . . palm to palm, cheek to cheek, foot to hand . . . tapping, scraping, rubbing.

★What sounds can you make more effectively with 20 people than on your own?

★Explore ways of working as a group to make sounds using only one part of the body . . .

GENTLY INTO MUSIC, Mary York, Longman Group UK Ltd

OURSELVES: Body Percussion
Hands

Chris's music

Chris, a boy with cerebral palsy, can put his hands 'in the middle' but he cannot make any sound. Boddi the clapping instrument is introduced to Chris . . . "I can trace round his shape with my hand and fingers" says Chris.

"Shall we paint a face on Boddi to look like you?" says Jo

Chris laughs when she does this!

"Can somebody make the clapping sound with Boddi when my hands are in the middle – I might need a supporting hand under my elbow and a voice to urge me on – Go slowly please" says Chris. "Next time I can play 'on cue', in that song we know, 'If you're happy and you know it'.

Centering hands together in midline is an early gross motor skill. We all have a psychological need to feel oneness.

Using a matching instrumental sound stimulates and reinforces the relevant body sound. Links of words and instrument shapes all strengthen the relationship. Letting Chris initiate his body sound at his pace before playing on cue is a good progression.

Saying "clap" and doing it with hands or an instrument has a matching feel with the word.

The hard quality of the guttural consonant 'c'(k) is like a bony sound. The outgoing short 'a' sound is like the energized action of clapping. The vowel changes to 'o' in clop, a rounded hollow shape in mouth, hands and instruments.

Take two hands that work and play, sound and sign and join my two sides making me a whole person.

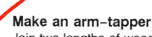

"BODDI"

use me as a template

Make an arm-tapper

Join two lengths of wood with a hinge joint for the elbow. Because of the differing bone-structure between the upper arm and forearm the sound varies . . . How? Try it!

Mirror paintings

To achieve symmetry in a variety of ways, complete an image by drawing or painting half a face, butterfly or tree and position a mirror to reflect the other half. Paint or splatter a picture and fold in half to make an ink-blob picture. Cut folded paper and use pieces to stick down in a symmetrical pattern.

WOODEN BODDIS (3 sizes) via PO Box 149, NG3 5PU

orchestral whip

butter pats

"Baddi"

Freddie Fish

castanets

CLAP

cream cartons

coconuts

CLOP

walnuts

yoghurt pots

dried oranges + lemons

Try your hand at conducting

Find "Uncle Tom" on the video [VN1.24]. Moving your arm from the elbow and with a bouncing wrist movement, start going down and up with the music. Feel the swinging two pulse and keep with it!

Now try three pulse. Find "The Swan" [VN1.22]. Moving your arm slowly and smoothly, make a triangle shape down and out and up.

Bonding Song

Tune: Name song
[VN1.1]
We're swaying and holding our hands
We're swaying and holding our hands
From side to side
From side to side
We're swaying and holding our hands

What other sounds can we make with our hands? What else can we do while we're swaying. Let's make a last verse getting slower and quieter.

And who is feeling tired?
And who is feeling tired?
We'll close our eyes
We'll close our eyes
And fall asleep . . .

★Jack chooses an instrument from the CLAP family.

★Jill chooses an instrument from the CLOP family.

★The leader asks them to find as many clap and clop sounds as they can for everyone to join in with, using body sounds.

★She explains the touch signal, ie "When you feel my hand on your shoulder – start playing: when you cannot feel it – stop playing."

★The group divides and the composition starts from silence – and finishes in silence.

★What happened when they played together?
Which bit was the most exciting?
Did Jill ever 'drown' Jack's sounds?
Well done everybody – lovely listening and playing.

Because this is an improvising role for Jack and Jill, make sure that exploration time has happened, ie we acquire vocabulary before we can speak.

The touch signal on the shoulder gives confidence in starting. Being non-visual it helps concentration and listening.

The guiding role of the leader helps to shape and phrase the composition.

Feeling part of a group all doing the same thing at the same time and noticing each other and each other's contributions, are good feelings.

Leader's role of noticing and commenting on a response can even include an unintentional one. "Safraz was blinking his eyes – that's a good idea. Can you show us Safraz? Can we include it?" We're swaying and blinking our eyes.

THE HAND AS A GUIDE TO LEARNING, Ester Cotton, Spastics Society, 12 Park Crescent, London W1N 4EQ

OURSELVES: Body Percussion
Feet

Ritual Instruments

In ancient times, stamping tubes included logs, sticks, bamboo and they were played by hitting the ground. These instruments are still used by women in connection with fertility rites in Asia, Africa and South America, to accompany the ritual dancing.

Our legs and feet, contacting the earth, make many different sounds. Treading grapes led to work songs, the foundations of dance. Bell sticks are used by Morris dangers. Walking sticks become extra legs.

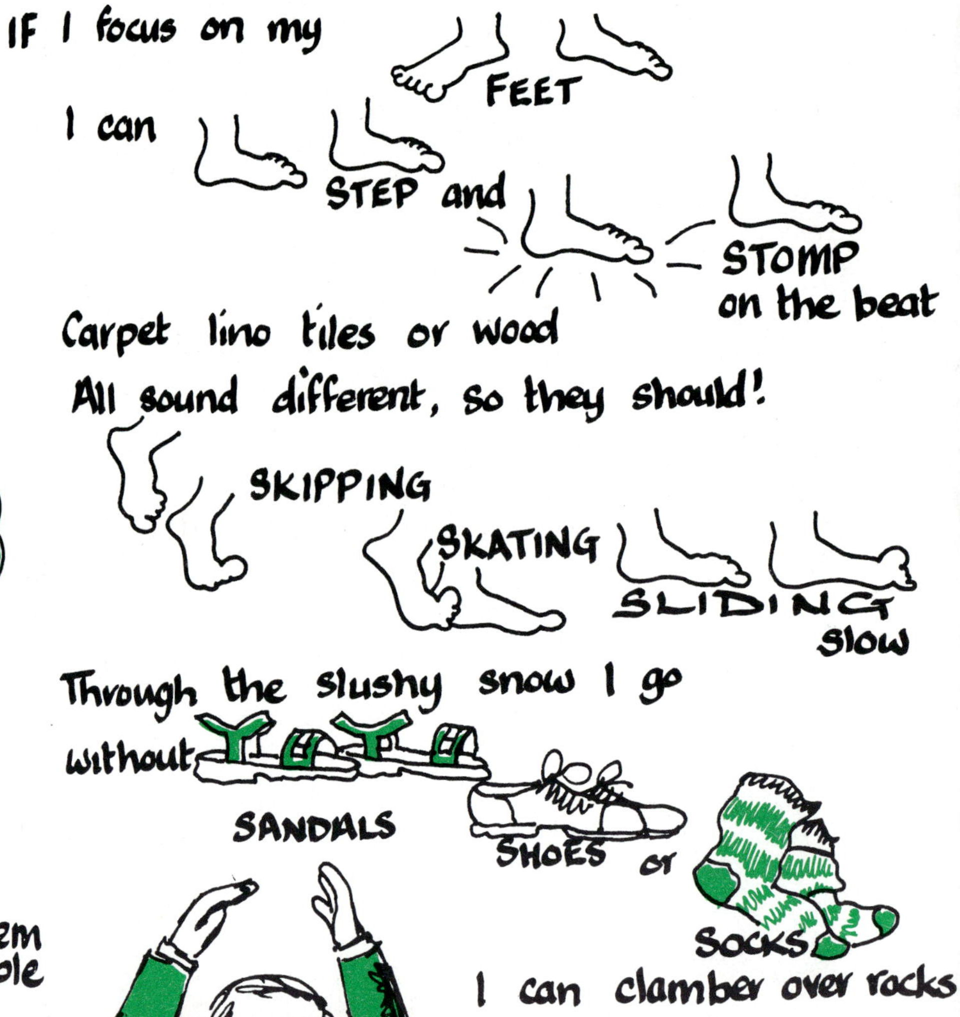

IF I focus on my FEET
I can STEP and STOMP on the beat
Carpet lino tiles or wood
All sound different, so they should!
SKIPPING SKATING SLIDING slow
Through the slushy snow I go
without SANDALS SHOES or SOCKS
I can clamber over rocks

tree

totem pole

twigs

stakes

stilts

walking stick

sword dancer

Fun for feet

★Find a variety of ways to use the jingle.

★Experiment with different foot surfaces, eg carpet, wood, tiles, felt.

★Sharpen up listening skills with guessing games behind a screen.

★Explore words and sounds beginning with 's' and 'sh' and reinforce with movement ideas.

Many words associated with feet sounds begin with 's' and 'sh', as do many dances!

Combining words and actions will give lots of practice in using these speech sounds

Samba Shimmy, Schottische, Sarabande, Sword dance

Growth of Ideas

The imagination is very fertile. Once you begin to feed it with ideas it generates many more of their own. You role lies in knowing how to capitalize on the ideas to stimulate the creativity of your group.

"I've just done a long slide" said Tim at the Pre–School video session. "So what do we call a long slide?" *Thinks* "Skate" said Tim. So we did, to the Skater's Waltz, and then we explored lots of sounds with our feet. After watching closely for contrasting sounds we listened to Dawn's sound.

(A strong rhythmic stamp)
"Let's all do it. What sort of a sound is it?" said the Leader. "Now let's listen to Brian's sound". (Gentle sliding in free rhythm).

"Let's make leg and feet instruments for Dawn and Brian" (cardboard tubes stuck into tissue boxes).

They stood in front of the group and moved their 'leg instruments' for us to copy with our real ones. When everyone had a pair of leg instruments we went stepping round the room, slithered on the floor like slimy snakes, and finished off with lots of stamps. We were not defeated!

Hands and Feet

★Everyone sits facing the conductor – Claire.

★Claire moves her hands up and down slowly and heavily, and asks everyone to use their feet. Stamping sounds get faster as Claire increases the speed of her hand movement. She pauses ⌒ and everyone rests.

★Claire has worked out ways of using her hands for feet shuffling, sliding, skating, toes tapping, heels hobbling. They are large clear movements which everyone can imitate using feet.

★Phil and Tracy come out next and divide the group in two. They find more sounds and the foot orchestra grows.

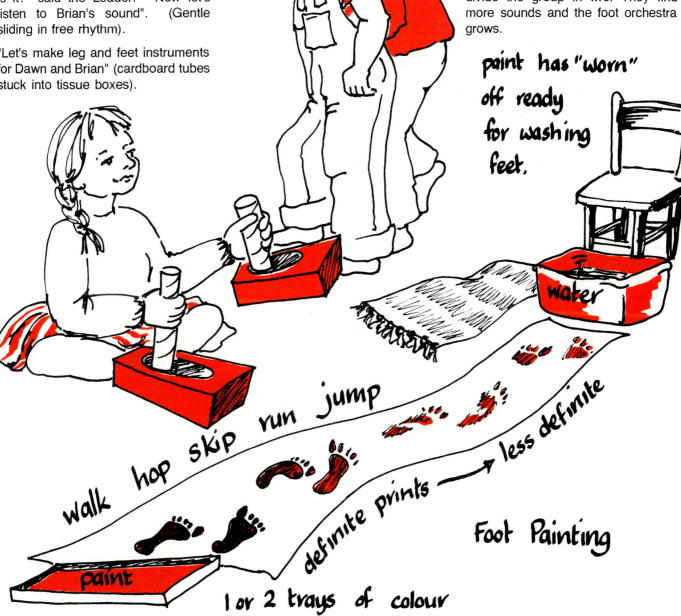

paint has "worn" off ready for washing feet.

water

walk hop skip run jump

definite prints ⟶ less definite

Foot Painting

paint

1 or 2 trays of colour

OURSELVES: Body Percussion
Knuckles and Knees

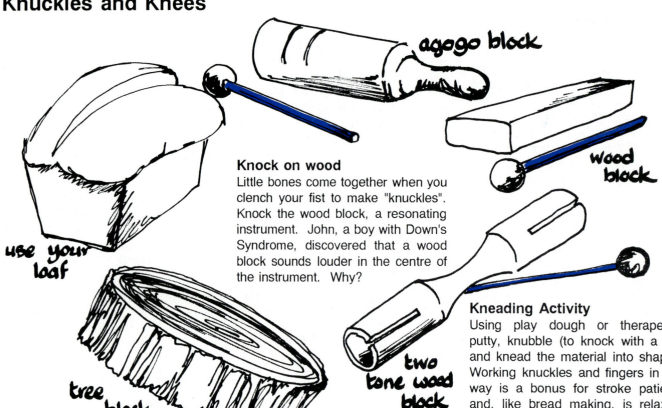

use your loaf

agogo block

wood block

two tone wood block

tree block

Knock on wood
Little bones come together when you clench your fist to make "knuckles". Knock the wood block, a resonating instrument. John, a boy with Down's Syndrome, discovered that a wood block sounds louder in the centre of the instrument. Why?

Kneading Activity
Using play dough or therapeutic putty, knubble (to knock with a fist) and knead the material into shapes. Working knuckles and fingers in this way is a bonus for stroke patients and, like bread making, is relaxing and creative. Don't forget the knitting too!

Know How
This fun family of bony knuckles, knees, knocking and cracking sounds, offers a knapsack of knockout activities.

Knuckle painting
Use large pieces of paper and sweeping movements with your knuckles to create various curves.

Is the paint different if the knuckles are knocked on the paper, or put down quietly or rolled?

Can you use your speaking or singing voice as you paint?

Make a picture with knuckle notes entitled "Knock on Wood". Can you include a knee blob?

Words to find sounds for
"Someone came knocking at my wee small door
Someone came knocking – I'm sure, sure, sure
I listened, I opened, I looked to left and right
But nought I heard a–stirring in the still dark night" Walter de la Mare

This old man he played three
He played knick knack on my knee
With a knick knack paddy whack
Give a dog a bone
This old man came rolling home

Words beginning with "kn" in the English language nearly all derive from Anglo–Saxon. The tongue in making an 'n' consonant "knocks" on the hard palate (the bony, gristly bit behind the top front teeth).

Guess what these objects are. They begin with "kn"

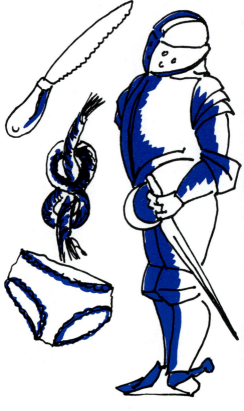

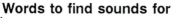

knuckle prints

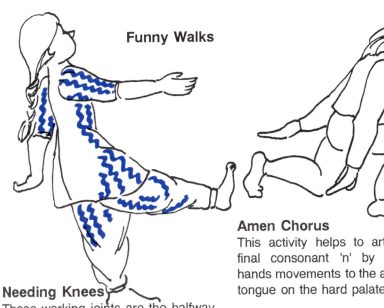

Funny Walks

Needing Knees

These working joints are the halfway house between the feet and the hips and are important in controlling the body's movements. As mobility hinges on the flexibility of the knees, here are some movement ideas to include in individual and group programmes. If they lead to some "Funny Walks" laughter, all the better.

★Floor sitting gives knee freedom so develop knee awareness by holding them.
●bending and straightening
●pressing together and pulling apart sideways
●knocking with knuckles, elbows or touching with chins.

★Taking the full weight of the body in kneeling can be painful for adults but children will enjoy sliding and walking on them using the hands as supports.

★Feet and legs then take the full weight and still holding the knees leads to knock-knees, goose-step walks, jelly legs and cross-overs. Pair work with one leading can begin the appreciation of the comedian's stock-in-trade, ie the comic walk. Look at John Cleese again.

★Knee high skipping moving into galloping and jumping starts the principle of working against gravity. Elevation is helped by strong elbow movement and additional height by the use of legs.

Amen Chorus

This activity helps to articulate the final consonant 'n' by linking the hands movements to the action of the tongue on the hard palate.

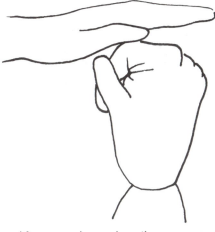

★After a deep breath, everyone chooses their own note and sings 'ah' on cue from the leader. (Encourage high and low sounds not just middle pitch, and an open mouth for a full vowel sound).

★On a second signal everyone sings 'meh' and ends with the 'n' consonant as the leader gestures.

★Repeat until the quality of sound is good and the placing of the final consonant is firm, together.

★Ask Katherine to come out, listen and comment on the performance and then take over from the leader.

★Standing on rostra and stools elevates the singers and the activity.

Use your loaf

Stale good quality bread and buns make worthy wood blocks for less dough than commercial ones! Spray on polyurethane varnish at regular intervals (three or four coats) until the outside is really hard. They do not last forever, but what does?

Overheard in a local baker's shop, showing off the bread block.
"I bought this loaf here and wanted you to see it transformed"
"But it's rock hard and very stale"
"Yes, it's three years old and still with us as a musical instrument"
"It says a lot for the quality of our bread"
"That's what I wanted you to appreciate"
Smiles all round . . .

Finish with a knees up

KNOCK ON WOOD, Multicultural Instruments and Workshops, Granary Wharf, The Canal Basin, Leeds LS1 4BR

OURSELVES: Body Percussion
Teeth and Nails

Grooves and notches

The scrape and scratch sounds of teeth and nails have interesting links in many areas; instruments, environment, language and feelings. Let's look at:

● teeth, which are notched surfaces within a resonating cavity, ie the mouth. This links with the guiro.

● nails (fingers and toes) – these are notched but not within a cavity. This links with the rezi–rezi.

● rib cage is a ridged bony surface. This links with Rosanna rib xylophone

● spinal column of linked vertebrae is another ridged bony surface. This links with the whirlie.

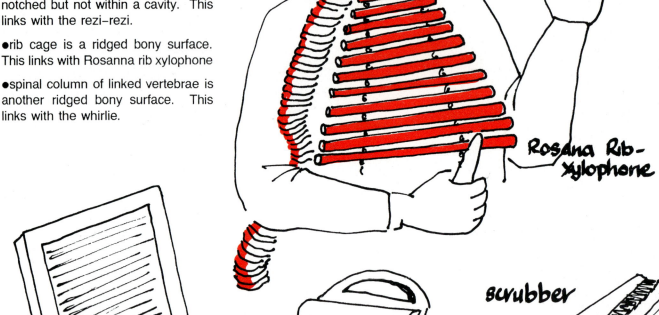

whirlie

guiro

Rezi - rezi

Rosana Rib-xylophone

skiffle board

scrubber

scraper

grater

The washboard was a scrubbing instrument in the days of the skiffle band. Make some for yourselves and play with a variety of scrapers.

Washboard (Mark 1)

★Cut and stick corrugated paper or bubble packing to pieces of firm card.

★Punch a hole at one end for a thumb–hold, or to thread a ribbon through and wear round the neck.

Washboard (Mark 2)

★Find scrap lengths of ribbed hardboard, often used for pelmets in DIY shops.

★Cut a thumb hole with a brace and bit 1/2–3/4" (12–18 mm) diameter, centrally, about 2" (50 mm) from one end.

★An optional handle can be stuck on the back using a small wooden door knob or a cotton reel.

Look at more scrubbers, scourers, graters and scratchers we find in the environment.

Combining Consonants

★Everyone needs a washboard and a scraper.

★Practise short taps . . . and long downward strokes

★Leader says "Potatoes can scrape and cats can scratch"

★Everyone repeats the jingle

★With short taps and long strokes, everyone accompanies the jingle on their washboard

★Leader asks everyone to say the jingle on its own, ie no washboard accompaniment. Is there any difference in the quality?

★Now add the accompaniment again and feel how saying, playing and moving achieves quality.

Most of the scraping sounds we make with our teeth and nails are very quiet. We amplify them by using like–sounding instruments. Find jingles, songs, proverbs, poems that can be used with the scraping family. "Scraping up sand from the bottom of the sea" could go well with corrugated shells and crustaceans. Sandpaper blocks are easy to make and sound very scrunchy.

Find objects from the environment that have corrugated or notched surfaces. Experiment with wood, plastic and metal scrapers to create a "crazy kitchen orchestra".

This practice of saying, playing and moving in a synchronized way is a bonus for those who find consonant clusters difficult. Joining up 's', 'c' 'r' needs energizing with breath, as the sounds groove over the tongue, forward/back/and forward with a rolling 'r'. Try it! It is the preparation breath and the physical action of playing that helps to 'connect' the consonants.

Practise short taps ⁊ ⁊ ⁊ ⁊ and downward strokes

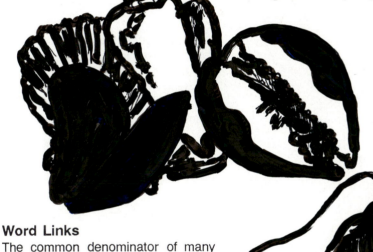

scrubbing brush

Scourer

Sandpaper block

Word Links

The common denominator of many words relating to the action and sound of grooved surfaces is the consonant cluster at the beginning, ie Scr, Gr, Cr. This happens in other languages. Here is the verb "to scrape" in

French: grater
German: kratzen
Romanian   scriznire

Scourer Painting

Using scourers, brushes etc. dip in a tray of paint. Print or scrape across the paper. What sound does it make? How many different textures can you create?

Finally the 'feeling' bit

Scratching can stimulate nerve ends and soothe physical irritations. But some scratching sounds can actually set up cerebral irritation. Grinding teeth, a violin, chalk on a blackboard. If 'rubbed up' in this way the irritation can be counteracted by a 'rub down' – with stroking, or a velvet glove?

OURSELVES: Body Percussion
Hollows

Historical drums

★A stretched skin over a hollow ... a membranophone ... a drum. Early civilizations used the earth as a symbolic drum; sending messages, communicating through vibration. Similarly the human body cavity below the navel, symbolized a drum but only the male was allowed to play the instrument.

Here are some activities that link the hollows of the body with words and instruments. Home-made drums are more suitable that commercial ones which are too resonant.

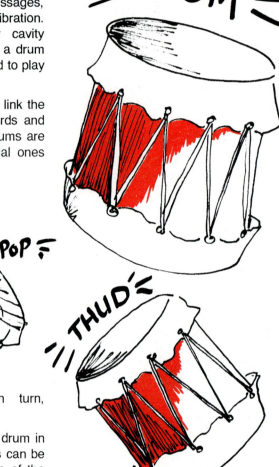

★Introduce each drum in turn, starting with the pop drum.

★Listen to everyone's cheek drum in turn. Pitched popping sounds can be made by changing the shape of the mouth and stretching the skin. Can anyone play a recognizable tune? Who can make the loudest `p' sound with their lips? a popissimo.

★Include the `pop' sound in `Ten fat sausages sizzling in a pan'.

★Fry some pop-corn for a poppin' experience. What other `pops' are there?

★Now take the 'pop' drum for everyone to copy-echo popping.

★The rounded shape of the mouth when saying 'pop' is like the rounded shape of the drum head. Even the vowel is round!
The skin of our cheeks and the drum is at tension and stretched over a hollow.

★Ask Oliver to come and play the `pop' drum for everyone to copy – echo popping with cheeks.

★Use the thud drum for similar exploration and games. Flat fingers produce a better sound than a fist.

★Finally the toom drum.

★Tune into VN3.2 and make a pop drum (cheeks) using half a coconut shell and Sellotape.

★Then make a thud drum and a toom drum [VN3.3]. Try to make a difference between the thud drum (chest) and the toom drum (tummy) with tin size and varieties of inner tube.

Now the leader uses all three drums for some listening games. "I play ... you look and listen ... then say the matching word and make the matching body-sound. i.e. pop, thud or toom."

"This time, I play and you listen with no looking. Which drum am I playing? Make the matching body sound. Now say the matching word but only mime the body sound".

★Develop the activity by mixing the sounds, setting up rhythmic patterns and inviting others to come and lead the activity.

Take time to introduce one drum at a time until recognition is secure. Auditory discrimination comes after auditory recognition ie "I can only tell the difference between the sounds if I know what those sounds are".

RECIPES: GRID NOTATION, Jan Holdstock, Lovely Music, Tadcaster, Yorkshire

Our body hollows are like drums and resonate at different pitches just like the vowels.

'O' (as in Pot)
POP
'U' (as in Putt)
THUD
`OO' (as in Put)
TOOM

Gato

Alto pan

Rhythm pan

waisted

Pellet

Tabla

Some drumming ditties

You will "Feel Happy and know it" when you revive this song that body parts can reach!

With our hands upon our tummy make a toom † † (twice)
With our hands upon our tummy it feels yummy, yummy, yummy
With our hands upon our tummy make a toom † †

With our hands upon our chest we have a thud † † (twice)
With our hands upon our chest, do you wear a woolly vest?
With our hands upon our chest we have a thud † †

Put our fingers on our cheeks and have a pop † † (twice)
Put our fingers on our cheeks, they are near the mouth that speaks
Put our fingers on our cheeks and have a pop † †

More drums to make

wine box liner 'toom' drum

soil pipe drum

cardboard tube drums

coffee tin bongos

King David and King Solomon† led
   Very merry lives – with
   Very many children and with
   Very many wives – but
   When old age came over them with
   Very many qualms – King Solomon wrote proverbs and King
   David wrote the psalms.

★Say the words with a strong bouncy rhythm over a firm four pulse.

★When it is secure, divide into two groups and say it as a round.
            Entry at †

★Everyone then prepares the accompaniment using speech and thigh–slaps on left and right sides L/R

Sol– o –mon Sol– o –mon Da – vid

L   R   R   L   R   R   L   R

Work slowly! Toss the pattern from side to side and then put on bongo drums.

★Divide into two groups
   (a) saying the verse
   (b) playing the accompaniment

Agree on a comfortable pace, get rid of your qualms and away you go. Swop the groups and take time to polish the proverbs and scintillate the psalms.

This verse needs the light treatment. Don't make it solemn!

The calypso pattern of "Solomon Solomon David" is the same as in the first section of the Rain Forest [VN2.9]. Fitting this syncopated accompaniment with the verse is the challenge.

Because the skills involved are rhythmic and physical, do work slowly.

Can you compose a melody?

OURSELVES: Body Percussion
The Head

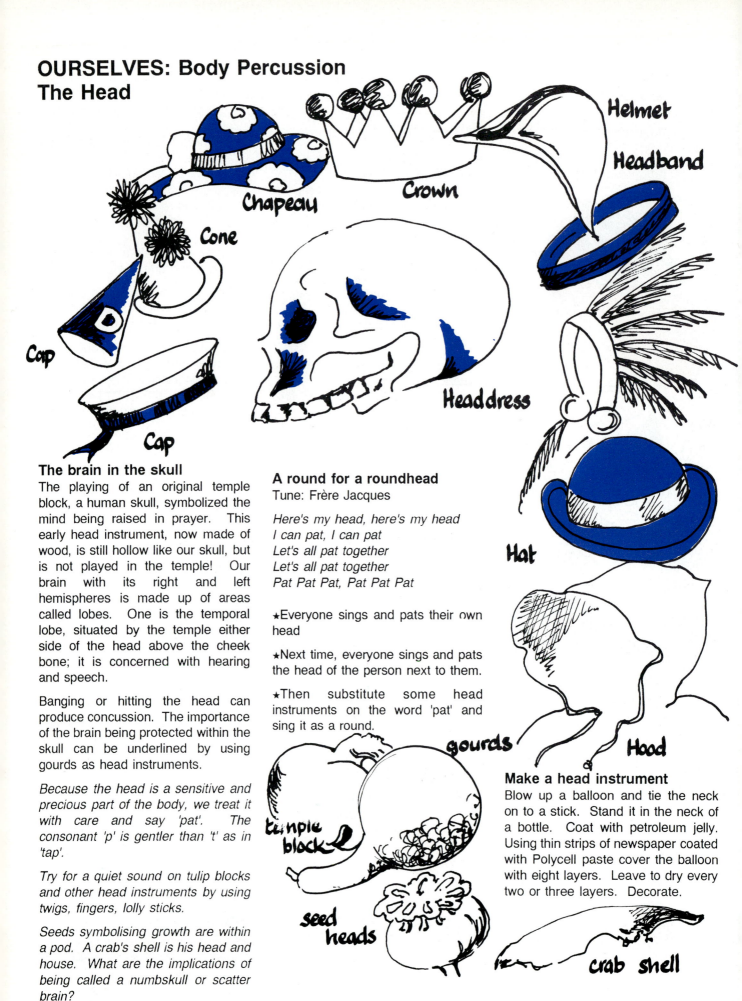

Chapeau

Crown

Helmet

Headband

Cone

Cap

Cap

Headdress

Hat

Hood

gourds

temple block

seed heads

crab shell

The brain in the skull

The playing of an original temple block, a human skull, symbolized the mind being raised in prayer. This early head instrument, now made of wood, is still hollow like our skull, but is not played in the temple! Our brain with its right and left hemispheres is made up of areas called lobes. One is the temporal lobe, situated by the temple either side of the head above the cheek bone; it is concerned with hearing and speech.

Banging or hitting the head can produce concussion. The importance of the brain being protected within the skull can be underlined by using gourds as head instruments.

Because the head is a sensitive and precious part of the body, we treat it with care and say 'pat'. The consonant 'p' is gentler than 't' as in 'tap'.

Try for a quiet sound on tulip blocks and other head instruments by using twigs, fingers, lolly sticks.

Seeds symbolising growth are within a pod. A crab's shell is his head and house. What are the implications of being called a numbskull or scatter brain?

A round for a roundhead
Tune: Frère Jacques

Here's my head, here's my head
I can pat, I can pat
Let's all pat together
Let's all pat together
Pat Pat Pat, Pat Pat Pat

★Everyone sings and pats their own head

★Next time, everyone sings and pats the head of the person next to them.

★Then substitute some head instruments on the word 'pat' and sing it as a round.

Make a head instrument
Blow up a balloon and tie the neck on to a stick. Stand it in the neck of a bottle. Coat with petroleum jelly. Using thin strips of newspaper coated with Polycell paste cover the balloon with eight layers. Leave to dry every two or three layers. Decorate.

EDU.K for KIDS Book on Educational Kinesiology (Whole Brain Learning), Dennison, via Kay Mc Carroll, 14 Golders Rise, London NW4 2HR

Nodding Hats
Tune: Jimmy Crack Corn

You've got to wear a hat like this
You've got to wear a hat like this
You've got to wear a hat like this
If you don't want to catch a cold.

★Everyone sings as the hat is passed round the circle, stopping at the end of the third line on the word 'this'.

★Chris, who is holding the hat, puts it on – everyone sings the fourth line feverishly!

★As everyone sneezes three times, getting louder each time, Chris tries to shake off the hat. He achieves this on the last sneeze – A–CHOO A–CHOO A–CHOO!

Wearing hats
Tune: "My little Augustin"

Sara's got the hat on,
The hat on, the hat on,
Sara's got the hat on,
and gives it to ⌒ Mike

★A brightly coloured plastic bowler is worn by Sarah who walks/dances round inside the group, waving or wearing the hat.

★At 'to' she looks for eye contact and waits to see who would like the hat.

★After "anticipation" time Sarah puts the hat on Wendy.

★Everybody sings/chants: "Wendy's got the hat on" and the game continues.

Nodding heads
★Start up a chant

Nod for yes and shake for no
Everyone can have a go
Shake for no and nod for yes
And leave the rest for us to guess

★Peter has prepared some fun questions

"Did you see Father Christmas yesterday?"

"Have you ever been in a hot air balloon?"
"Are you wearing shoes?"

★Anyone who has a question, gives a signal at the end of the chant and asks their question when given a nod by Peter

Precious heads
Helen says:
"Jenny has a lovely head. At the front she has a forehead with blonde hair growing from her scalp. Can I stroke your hair, Jenny?"

Comment on texture, colour and style.

"Stroke the head instrument, Jenny, and feel the round shape – just like your head."

For those with cerebral palsy, touching the head and back of the neck is inappropriate because of

involuntary spasm. Working face to face can establish trust and smiles, as well as benefitting feeding programmes, eye contact and balance. You're in position for a hug too!

Stroking messages are close to massages – sensory communication at its best.

Because of a brain lesion, Jenny (aged 15) has uncontrollable limb movement. This form of cerebral palsy is called athetosis.

Using a head instrument, Jenny learns about her head through touch, ie shape and similarity of head to head instrument. John guides Jenny's hands (or hand) over the head instrument while Annie mirrors these movements on Jenny's head.

The gourd fits into the gaps of a plinth table.

Specific problems within brain damage often manifest themselves in head–lolling and head–banging. The latter can be seen as an attempt to make contact with the brain, ie self–stimulation.

OURSELVES: Body Percussion
Hair and Whiskers

The family of strings –
CORDOPHONES – one or more
strings or wires stretched across a
sound box and set in vibration .....

By PLUCKING AND BOWING

piano

by STRIKING with a HAMMER

or WIND BLOWING through them

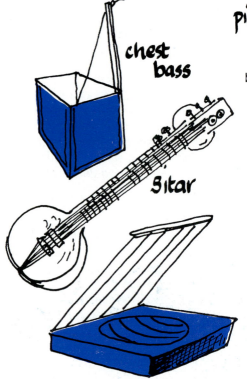

chest bass

Sitar

Egg slicer

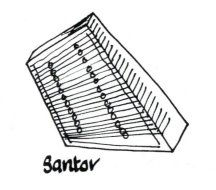

dulcimer

Santor

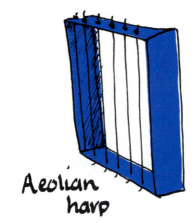

Aeolian harp

*Pluck, and plick, are short dry
sounding words. Listen to your hair
as you pluck one or two strands.
Experiment stretching string and
elastic bands. Plucking a stringed
instrument is called 'pizzicato'.*

ZITHERS
*Stroking the strings of a chromaharp
or autoharp feels and sounds
wonderful. Watch Alison, Maureen
and Pat on the video, finger-pressing
the chord buttons and strumming on
the other hand.*

*The Omnichord is an electronic
version of the above. With built-in
rhythms and minimal touch effort it
gives maximum sound rewards and
lots of chords.*

Twangler Mark I
Insert an elastic band or piece of
string into the solid end of a yoghurt
pot and tie a knot inside.

Twangler Mark II
Get off-cuts of downpipe from DIY
shops, varying in length and
diameter. Sandpaper the edges.
Cover the top with Fablon then round
the sides. Use a mason's plumb line
instead of string.

*Experiment with a transducer to
amplify the sounds (page 46). One
strand of hair is transformed.
Twangler Mark II can be used as a
friction drum by scraping your nails
along the string. Vibrations travelling
through solid material sound strong
because of the amplification.*

Whiskers and beards – a hairy song – with no tune – Can you write one?

*I have a dear old Grandad
For whom I nightly pray
He has a set of whiskers
That are always in the way.*

*Around the supper table
We make a merry group
Until dear Grandad's whiskers
Get tangled in the soup.*

*When Grandad goes in swimming
No bathing suit for him
He ties his whiskers round his waist
And gaily plunges in.*

*Grandad in a tavern
He likes his lager beer
He puts his clothes peg on his nose
To keep his whiskers clear*

String painting

Dip a length of cord/string in paint and draw across a sheet of paper. Experiment with different hand and finger movements, sizes of paper and string thicknesses. Swirly patterns that evolve relate to free rhythm (no pulse) and free flow experience in movement.

Pretend there is a string painting on the floor.

Following the pathway, travel in many ways – forwards and backwards, curling and twisting, singing a meandering melody as you go.

Which body part is leading? My elbows, fingers or head? What levels, ie planes am I moving in? High, low or medium?

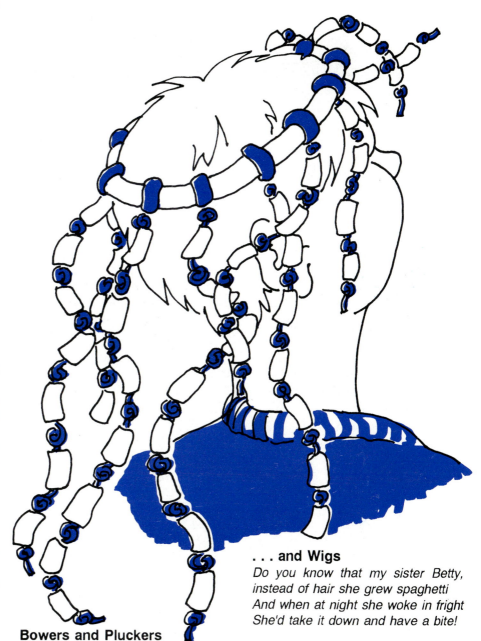

Bowers and Pluckers

BOWING a violin or 'cello produces a long sustained sound called 'legato'. Pretend to bow a 'cello and say 'bow' as you go. The 'oh' vowel will last as long as your breath does! Listen to The Swan [VN1.22]

Do you remember the musical saw?

Do you remember Shirley Abicair playing the zither? The Harry Lime theme? She plucked the tune with one hand and an accompaniment with the other.

. . . and Wigs

Do you know that my sister Betty, instead of hair she grew spaghetti And when at night she woke in fright She'd take it down and have a bite!

apologies to OGDEN NASH

After making a macaroni wig, Anisha said to her Rastafarian friend. "Oh Good, I look just like you now."

Thread macaroni on lengths of nylon blind cord knotting after each piece. Loop ends over metal ring (approx 1" /25 mm diameter) and stitch. Psychedelic paint can give colour and shine.

Hair, strings, laces, make plaits and pony-tails. Decorated with beads they enhance our image.

OURSELVES: Body Percussion
Hot Pot

SWITCH

① leader

players

② leader

players

③ leader

players.

Pointing fingers

Tune: Here we go round the Mulberry Bush

★David sings:
This is the way my finger points
finger points finger points
This is the way my finger points
Where's it going to stop?

★On the word 'stop' everyone calls out the name of the person who is being pointed at. It's Fatima.

★Fatima sings
"This is the way etc" and points to everyone in turn until the word 'stop' and the game continues.

Keeping a finger on the pulse is the point of this game and encourages

- different directions for pointing, ie clockwise/anti-clockwise/random

- different fingers being used – Peter Pointer invites Ruby Ring to join in

- anticipation and participation

Playing Fingers

Wiggle your fingers, one by one
Tap your fingers, two by two
Thrum your fingers, three by three

Flap your fingers, four by four
Fly your fingers, five by five

Note the similar consonantal beginnings 'w' (wiggle and one) etc.

Dramatize the first 'action' word with a fun high and low voice and some repetition, ie wiggy, wiggy, wiggle. This will avoid a sing-song metric rhythm developing. Let the creativity happen by not always 'showing how'. How many ways can you "thrum" your fingers?

Play a game – SWITCH [VN1.16]

1★Feeling a steady pulse Bobby starts making a repeated body sound. Everyone joins in. When he calls SWITCH he changes to another body sound and everyone changes too. Bobby introduces a new body sound – the rump bump!

2★Start off the same way. Then choose a different body sound. Nobody changes until SWITCH is called. For a short time the leader and the group are making different sounds.

3★Clare starts on her own – everyone watches but doesn't join in. On SWITCH they do what they've looked at and listened to. Immediately Clare begins a new sound. She then calls SWITCH and everyone does her second sound, ie the class were always one behind Clare.

Finding where your head and feet are and playing them in time is demanding. Give time for action to be absorbed, before calling SWITCH.

Keep body sounds at one level to start with, eg hands. Extend by 'jumping' levels gradually. Moving from feet to head is an advanced co-ordination skill for some.

Include some movement (giving welcome silences!) and whistles, whoops and warbles.

Ring the changes and say SCHIMBA (pr. Skimba), Romanian for SWITCH.

Use a FUN WHISTLE too.

Swaying Sailors

Tune: What shall we do with the drunken sailor
Everybody sways and sings:

What can we do when we're in a circle
What can we do when we're in a circle
What can we do when we're in a circle
Who is going to show us?

★Leader watches responses and everyone joins in with the one selected

We can stamp our feet together
We can stamp our feet together
We can stamp our feet together
Stamp our feet together

★Repeat *"What can we do etc"* for next solo response

In the Whirlie ring activity [VN1.6] everyone participated within the security of the circle, still retaining their individuality. In Swaying Sailors, each person has an opportunity to show an idea and then share it with the group.

DR KNICKBOCKER, Thompson and Winfield, Beaters Series, Schott Ed.12163

Body Sound Round

Tune: London's Burning.   Not too fast!

Stamp Stamp Slap Slap
Stamp Stamp Slap Slap†
Toom Thud Thud
Toom Thud Thud
Pat Pat
Pat Pat
Pat-a-Thud Thud
Toom Slap Slap

★Everyone follows the leader making body sounds and singing the words.

    Stamp (foot) Slap (thighs)
    Toom (tummy) Thud (chest)
    Join up Pat and Thud (Head to chest) by touching shoulders

★Choose the ending you prefer. Going down to thighs (as above) or repeating Pat-a-thud or having them both for a bit of harmony!

★Try it without words!

★Making group circles, sing it as a round
    †Entry for voices

★Ask Susan and Saffiya to come out and listen and comment

★*Find words to make a repeated pattern (ostinato) that could accompany this Body Sound Round.*

eg   *†*

Let my feet go stamp

(The repeat sign at the beginning and end means keep going)

Put this speech pattern on to some 'gentle' instruments.
Be ready to get everyone "IN" with foot sound and stamp stamp at †
A tricky entry!

Find a matching 'instrument' for each body sound. Can you find one for the thigh slap? The metallic sounds of callipers are a bonus in this activity!
An instrumental interlude would make a different 'middle' if you wanted to make a sandwich – A B A

Mixing 'ingredients', ie body sounds and words, and basing them on a known 'recipe' ie familiar tune, gives security and scope for variations.

Matching the rise and fall of the tune, to the up and down of the physical actions, reinforces the concept of pitch.

Using only Body Sounds gives experience of internalizing speech. It also produces a new sound texture which heightens 'listening'!

Rhyme Time.   Senses and Nonsenses to play with

I smell a rose with my nose
I taste some chips on my lips
I look at flies with my eyes
I touch the sand with my hand
I hear a cheer with my ear
I see a flea scratching my knee

Copy Cats

★Sarah walks into the middle of the circle and either makes a gesture or takes up a pose. She then returns to her place.

★Everyone tries to do exactly the same thing, in the same manner and using the same voice.

★Anyone who wishes may take a turn.

This is a development from [VN1.2]. Sarah's role is an improvising one. Careful observation, seeing how others see you and breaking with your own customary way of moving, in your attempts to imitate another person, are all outcomes of this simple activity.

SEVENTY SIMPLE SONGS WITH OSTINATI, Albert Chatterley, Novello

OURSELVES: Body Percussion
Finger Theatre

ROLL UP ROLL UP..

FOR THE FABULOUS FINGER THEATRE

Using fingers and hands only, marvel at the shapes and images you can make.........
a flower opening, birds, fish, raindrops, tying a bow, unwrapping a gift.

Saying HELLO GOODBYE YES NO.........

and much, much more.........
Open the door to dramatic digital dexterity

COMING SOON TO A HAND NEAR YOU.

OURSELVES: Voice

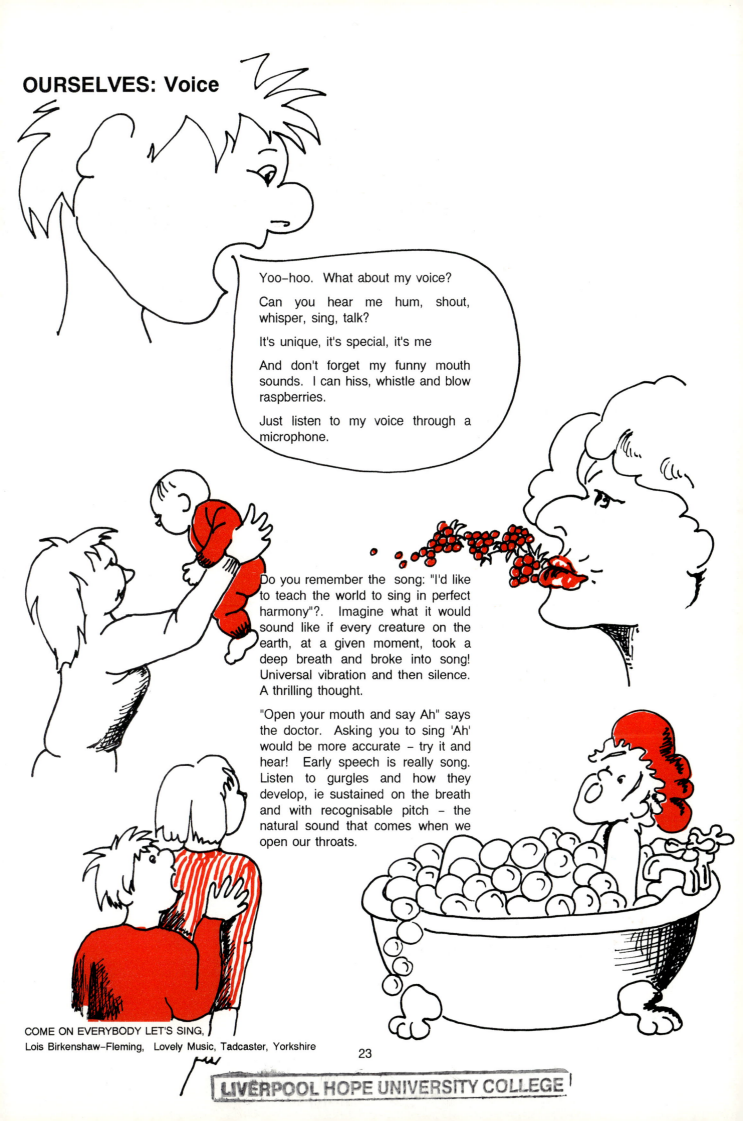

Yoo-hoo. What about my voice?

Can you hear me hum, shout, whisper, sing, talk?

It's unique, it's special, it's me

And don't forget my funny mouth sounds. I can hiss, whistle and blow raspberries.

Just listen to my voice through a microphone.

Do you remember the song: "I'd like to teach the world to sing in perfect harmony"?. Imagine what it would sound like if every creature on the earth, at a given moment, took a deep breath and broke into song! Universal vibration and then silence. A thrilling thought.

"Open your mouth and say Ah" says the doctor. Asking you to sing 'Ah' would be more accurate – try it and hear! Early speech is really song. Listen to gurgles and how they develop, ie sustained on the breath and with recognisable pitch – the natural sound that comes when we open our throats.

COME ON EVERYBODY LET'S SING,
Lois Birkenshaw-Fleming, Lovely Music, Tadcaster, Yorkshire

OURSELVES: Voice
The Vulnerable Voice

Talking it over

Of all the sounds we make ourselves, the human voice, in both speaking and singing, is the most powerful means of communication; it is also the most vulnerable. Losing one's voice for physical or psychological reasons can be traumatic; mutism and speech problems can also indicate rejection as a result of physical, verbal and sexual abuse. The self-rejection so often voiced "But I can't sing", applies to many. Sadly some of the reasons for this still survive.

Whirlies are a passport to vocal play at all times, p 54-55.

★Response to child's singing attempts, "Stop that noise"

★Advice(!) given at school "Mouth the words but don't sing"

★Result "I'm tone-deaf".

Let's explode the last-mentioned myth

★*Ask someone to play two notes i.e. tones on a piano or other pitched instrument.*

★*Listen. If you can hear that they are different you are not tone deaf.*

★*If you can differentiate between tones that are near each other, your hearing is excellent.*

So you are not tone-deaf, just lacking in confidence.

Here are some ideas for you to try out on your own and then with your group. Remember that your loss, if you don't share your singing voice is a much greater loss for your children and clients. With some stroke patients it is possible to awaken residual speech through song, and an elective mute will often choose to sing rather than speak.

Reluctant vocalizers will find their voices with a microphone.

Tune in with the speaking voices that urge and encourage movement effort with special needs children [VN1.21].

Carry a kazoo with a string round your neck. Pierce the under part of the kazoo at the wide end with a hot needle. Thread and wear. "Doo Doodelly Doo- you can play a kazoo".

Buy some whistles, train, duck, swanee, for your personal play. They are wonderful laughter-starters.

Read one of the poems aloud, from the Music of Poetry, p 32.

Then sing along with Uncle Tom [VN1.23].

Collect cardboard tubes for jazz trumpets and play along with the Dedworth Blues [VN3.15]. There are ideas for improvising your own blues too.

Try the sounds of the steam engine [VN1.19]

THE SINGING CURE, Paul Newham, Random House, 7c Ballards Lane, London N3 1UX

OURSELVES: Voice
Breathing In

How it works

The singing voice is the most personal instrument of all. It is 'born' in the voice box, a complex muscular mechanism which sounds out (or not!) how we feel. Situated between head and body, the voice box can be the link between thought and feeling. This 'sounding out' comes from within the deep recesses of the psyche.

To get the best out of your voice, you need to relax first.

★Loosen up by having a good shake, laughing, jigging around.

★Have another dip into the 'Starters' on page 2

★Have some silly songs or limericks or jokes ready.

Here is a fun way of raising awareness of breathing:

★Imagine you are a washing machine with no water in it.

★Placing your hands on your tummy and holding your mouth like the tube of the water pipe, suck in the air in short bursts and feel your tummy getting bigger and bigger. Hold it still and then . . .

★Blow the water out through the pipe as the machine empties. Feel this with your hands on tummy.

★Repeat this with someone helping you to FEEL the filling process through your back.

★Hands are placed at the base of the rib cage. Keep them rounded with fingers and thumb close together. The touch needs to be firm, as the hands are acting as a marker, ie "I can feel where the bottom of the washing machine is. That's the bit I need to fill first".

OURSELVES: Voice
Sounding out

Thoughts and actions

After breathing in, we breathe out and make sound. Are you a vibrating agency? Find out with these resonant reminders.

★Make a circle inside your mouth and close your lips. Put one finger on your lips and HUM

'Ommm'

Feel wise and rounded like a old BUDDHA . . . and FREE . . . with your brain and blood flow belonging to YOU and no-one else.

★Feel similar vibrations by touching your nose with one finger and HUM

'Nnnn'

★Imagine you step out of a caravan into the morning air and sunlight. There is blue sky. You pulsate with excitement and you know it feels good. Open your mouth wide with a relaxed jaw and SING

'AH'

★Put your hand on your Adam's Apple and with an open mouth make a rasping sound to 'HA'. As you sing different notes, you feel the difference in vibration. This self-expression area relates closely to emotional sounds – groan, moan, scream etc.

Whichever box we put ourselves in, as singers, sounding out in any and every way is vital to well being. Opening up our voices releases, invigorates and changes our vision.

Pick up a phone and sing opera or rugby songs – loudly.

Go to a voice workshop.

Believe in the benefits enough to use these ideas with your groups.

Voice sounds, images and colours form some of the energy wheels known as chakras. Opening up and balancing these energies helps us to flow in harmony with our total being.

The Hee-Hi-Ho-Yoo Chorus

★Vera stands in front of the group, raises her hand and sings HI. Circles fingers (polo mint) and sings HO, points to a fellow and sings HE, points to everyone and sings YOO, flattens her hands and HUMMM!

★Connie makes action/sound for a road-drill d-d-d-d
bubbling water b-b-b-b
symposium of snakes s-s-s-s

This joining-in activity develops vowel and consonant sounds and is of special value for those who have limited articulation. Stimulated by gesture it encourages sounding-out within the security of a group.

Wind in the Willows

★Everyone explores wind sounds, ie moaning, whistling, howling, wet.

★Talk about why and how they are different (shape of the mouth-tongue position).

★Have groups of moaning winds – whistling, howling

★Sanjay comes out to conduct his wind band.

★Sanjay brings in the groups one by one using gesture and eye contact and mixing them in different ways.

This activity is excellent for a windy day. Add whirlies too. Stimulate by singing into the back and blowing on parts of the body.

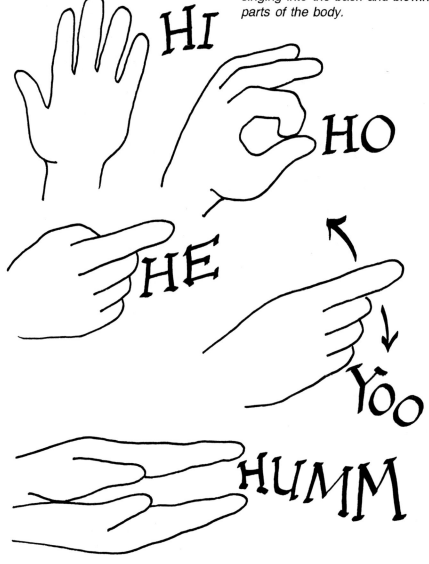

COURSES IN VOICE MOVEMENT THERAPY, Led by Paul Newham. Contact Tonny Grey, Tel. 081 343 1959

OURSELVES: Voice
More sounding out

★Lis is the conductor and points at the sounds written on the flip chart.

★Everyone responds with an appropriate vocal sound.

★Lis asks for repeated sneezes and she indicates high and low laughter by using her other hand up and down at different levels. She limits screams!

★Everyone takes turns. New sounds are included.

★Discussion re responses and development of the activity throw up lots of suggestions, ie division of groups, solo spots, building a voice collage?

This can be a way of helping a non-speaker to make acceptable sounds that are not speech or song.

Mouth sounds
Do you remember the hisses, boings and other steam engine sounds [VN1.19] that became a trigger for the movement sequence [VN2.7]. The voice sounds came first. Their variety and quality were mirrored in the movement. This was a safe but fruitful way of working and showed some growth points.

Sometimes a voice 'opener' for a sighted group could start like this:

No place to go
★Everyone sits on the ground in a circle, except for Paddy who remains on the outside.

★A chant begins "Poor Paddy hasn't got a place. Oh what a shame".

★The chant can be taunting or sympathetic. It can be elaborated on as long as it keeps going.

★Paddy walks round the circle until he says out loud "Oh yes I have" and takes Sean and Teresa by the shoulders and moves them out of the circle. Paddy then takes one of their places.

★Sean and Teresa, who have been thrown out, shake hands, cross and travel around the outside of the circle. They shake hands again as they meet, and then both run for the one place left.

★Sean gets it, so Teresa is left out and the game continues as the chant starts up again.

This game can be played for vocal and physical exercise.

Introducing ideas of exclusion, justice and injustice and homelessness can be played out with loud verbal assertiveness.

To experience the feeling of exclusion while playing a game in which the winner of each round does not get to play the game.

WHEN WORDS SING, Murray Schafer, Universal

OURSELVES: Voice
Soundings from the inner self

Ways and means
Strong emotions and tensions which have built up inside people need to be released and diffused. Knowing how and when to intervene is a skill which comes with experience and understanding. These suggestions have worked in particular situations and could be adapted. You won't always get it right the first time, but keep trying!

A Talking Tent
Tom never spoke. He just made loud disturbing sounds. One day he arrived in a very angry mood.

"Would you like to go into the talking tent, sit on the red cushion, and tell the instrument (a sansa) how you feel?

After a few minutes, a volcano of expletives erupted from the talking tent. Kate joined him with her sansa. "That's what people call you, isn't it Tom?"

"Yes" he shouted. "Shall we sit down and tell the instruments how we feel?" said Kate. We did. He always wanted to visit the talking tent after that.

We made a big talking instrument for Nisar from a tea chest with bicycle spokes. He played it with his feet.

Music for the Elderly – Tibble Trust – Queen's Hospital, Croydon
"Nobody needed any sleeping pills that night" said the ward sister after an evening of song. Lit by visuals on an overhead projector, the ceiling became a sky of colour and images. Daisy rode her tandem. "What shall we sing next?" was a guessing game from the picture.

Talking fingers
The African instrument called a SANSA (or Mbira) or THUMB PIANO has talking fingers made of metal, and makes CLICK and FLICK sounds – short vowel with quick dry consonants. Each African tribe is recognised by its random scale which is produced by differing lengths of metal in a specific order.

A MUSIC BOX is in the same family, the tongues moving over a cylindrical drum. Sweet talk tunes make one listen.

BOB – aged 35 years in a hospital for people with profound and multiple learning disabilities
"He always just lay there. Nobody took much notice. Sometimes he made a groaning sound. When he started I tried to pitch my HUM with his sound. Eventually we came together. Between his shoulders, I hummed and sang into his back – one tone – resonating him with sound – a sort of sonic bath. A helper continued the sound while I ran to get my equipment. We amplified it, recorded it and played it back to him – HIS SOUND. This was the foundation TONE. We began building.

★Everyone gathered round Bob humming and singing different vowel sounds – short sounds and long sounds – reinforcing with touch – taps for short sounds, strokes for long ones.

★By moving an appropriate limb, gently up and down, we gradually changed the pitch to match the up and down movement.

★We sang songs on Bob's note – about him – commenting on his physical appearance – eye colour, etc.

★Monotone songs (on one note) are never monotonous if the lyric is praising and not patronising

Bob enjoyed being the centre of attention – we had made contact with his inner self.

"That was lovely!" said Pat after Michael's song [VN3.13]. Michael KNEW it had been good. He'd sung final notes at phrase endings, felt supported by the accompaniment and enjoyed the song for its own sake.

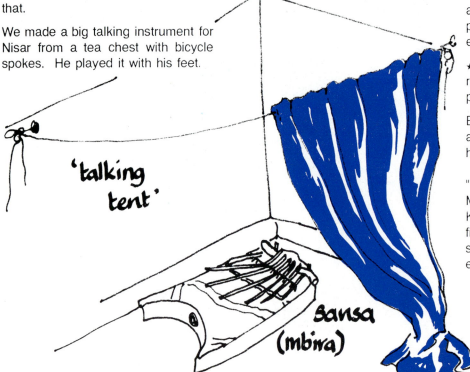

'talking tent'

sansa (mbira)

NURSING IN TUNE WITH MUSIC (Video), Deakin University DUX 228 Australia. Cert no. NPR305V01

OURSELVES: Voice Improvisation

Communication through song

In one-to-one sessions with special needs children, channels of communication can be opened up with vocal improvisation. Using a tune you know, make up a running commentary song about what is happening.

Tune: Here we go round the Mulberry Bush

"Mark is walking round the room, round the room, round the room, Mark is walking round the room and now he's going to stop"

Sing about everything you observe, make pauses for stillness and fill in with la-las if necessary. Be aware of the complexity of your language. Try not to 'flood' with too many concepts at once. It may need to be as simple as "walking, walking, walking – stop". Speed up and slow down with Mark; try not to lead with action. He needs to be re-assured of your level of involvement; facial expression and body language will say so much. You may choose to use your singing voice quite freely i.e. not based on a song; or support yourself with a light accompaniment on a chromaharp, guitar or keyboard. (This principle of 'going-along-with' see p52 can rivet the attention of the withdrawn, or those with problems of autism).

Singing about everything

To be sung to, is one of the most personal lines of communication; it says more than words can. This call and response activity is a fun way of enticing people to 'sing out' about themselves; their feeling and fears ... and sometimes their secrets! Making an individual response within the safety of a group, gives everyone a sense of security. Before having a go with your group, try out some ideas in private. Remember to pitch your voice at a level which is comfortable for you and your group. Accompany yourself with a guitar, chromaharp or tuned percussion. Try C and G playing them together (alto range preferable) as a support to your singing voice and as a punctuation stop.

"Hello – my name is Father Christmas" (strum or plonk)
"I am very old" (strum or plonk)
"My favourite colour is red" (strum or plonk) "and I love chips" (strum or plonk)

Everyone will love it!
When you feel confident to have a go with your group, sing about anything you like on one note.

Here are some suggestions.

★Sing "Hello" – and wait for the response
Sing it again...

★Sing "Is the sun shining today"? for a YES or NO response.
"Do you like curry"? for a YES and NO response.

★Treat them to your practised "My name is ..." etc.

★Then sing questions in the same sequence
"How old are you"?
"What is your favourite colour"?
"Do you like chips?"

★With everyone gaining confidence (and you can feel this happening) sing to one person ... and then another.

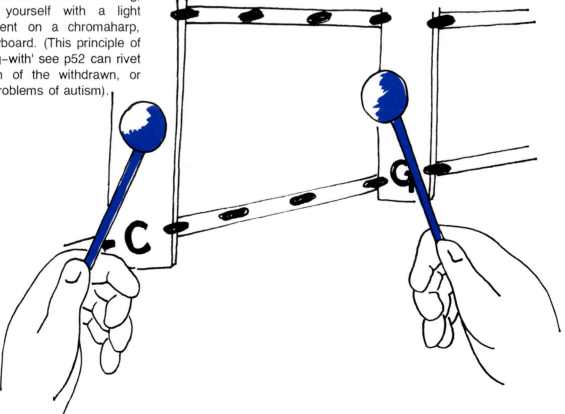

OURSELVES: Voice
"You Can't See"

A game to encourage singing improvisation

★Everyone sits or stands in a circle.

★Hank is blindfolded and stands in the centre.

★The leader starts a singing chant in one or two notes and everyone joins in.

"You can't see so you must use your ears
Can you hear who's singing now?"

★During the chant the leader turns Hank to face a player – Amy – but of course he can't see her.

★Hank sings a short question to Amy who sings an answering phrase.

★Hank has to guess who answered.

★If Hank guesses correctly Amy comes in to the centre and is blindfolded. Everyone sings the chant.

★If Hank does not guess it is Amy he sings another question for her to answer or gives in.

The singing voice is the most personal instrument of all. Initially the leader can sing a question for Hank until he is confident enough to sing for himself. Reluctance to sing will usually disappear as familiarity with the game grows.

Silence is a vital part of music. If someone does not wish to sing, treat this as a positive contribution.

It is so important that everyone is encouraged and never criticised, however tentative their contributions. Be aware that even a slight facial expression can convey criticism and may inhibit that person from singing again for weeks, months or longer.

POMPALEERIE JIG, Thompson & Baxter, Thomas Nelson & Sons Ltd

OURSELVES: Voice
The Potting Shed

★Through the same window another creature arrives.
"WHAT IS IT? WHAT DOES IT SOUND LIKE?"

★As it gets hot the wood walls contract and there are spaces between the slats. Some things come in.
"WHAT ARE THEY? WHAT DO THEY SOUND LIKE?"

★The gardener opens the door, we can now hear sounds from outside.
"WHAT SOUNDS CAN WE HEAR? WHAT DO THEY SOUND LIKE?"

★At this point it starts to rain.
"WHAT DOES THIS SOUND LIKE?"

★We shut the door and no longer hear the sounds outside.

★Some of the creatures creep away and others find quiet hiding places.

★The wood expands, the walls are shut.

★All other creatures leave and we finally shut the window.

ALL IS QUIET

Making a sound picture

This outline of a dialogue, with the partially sighted in mind, can be an imaginative stimulus for any group.

Internal visual imagery is awakened by the questions and a mental picture is built by the sharing of answers. The scene could be anywhere – an attic, a cellar, a forest, inside an Egyptian tomb.

All is quiet and still. There is a door and open window. It starts to get hot so we open the window.

★Something gets in.
"WHAT IS IT? WHAT DOES IT SOUND LIKE?"

OURSELVES: Voice
The music of poetry

Finding links

Music and poetry both consist of organized patterns of sound. They also have meaning to which we respond with feeling and imagination. They share certain basic elements which can be used to achieve different effects. Here are some ways of using poetry to explore these different building blocks.

Timbre (tone colour)

What sort of sound do we want?

Take a poem that described sounds and use it as a stimulus for composing

The cat sat asleep by the side of the fire, (very quiet sounds)
Her mistress snored loud as a pig (scraping sounds)
Jack took up his fiddle, by Jenny's desire,
And struck up a bit of a jig (any tuned instrument)

Using sound effects, ie one sound imitating another, is another starting point for exploration and sequencing.

Duration

Some sounds are long, some are short. A series of same length sounds gives a steady beat or pulse. Combinations of different length sounds give varying rhythmic patterns.

Slow, Peter,
Slow, Peter
Take your time to go.
Taste, savour,
Taste, savour,
Nothing's gained by haste

Explore the long short short rhythm of the repeated lines on different instruments.

Saying words can help underpin the playing of rhythmic patterns.

Listen to Beethoven's use of a similar pattern in the slow movement of his 7th Symphony.

Textures

Using different ones will add spice. How many layers of sound shall we have?

Pease Pudding hot
Pease Pudding cold
Pease Pudding in the pot
Nine days old

★Repeat the words "Nine Days Old". Add an untuned instrument and accompany the poem with this pattern.

Say the poem. Clap the rhythm. Play the rhythm on untuned instruments.

Say the poem. Clap the rhythm. Play the * pattern accompaniment.

If your group can add all these ingredients together you have made a tasty two-part texture.

Can you use other words from the rhyme in a similar way to achieve a three-part texture?

Pace

Use body percussion, found sounds or untuned percussion to accompany a fast rendering of

Tom, Tom, the piper's son
Stole a pig and away he run!
The pig was eat and Tom was beat
And Tom went roaring down the street

Listen to Rimsky Korsakov's "The Flight of the Bumble Bee", Ravel's "Pavan for a Dead Infanta"
and contrast with the slow pattern of sound of:

A wise old owl sat in an oak
The more he saw, the less he spoke
The less he spoke, the more he heard
Why can't we all be like that wise old bird?

What about the effect achieved by a gradual change of pace? Try "The song the Train Sang" by Neil Adams (Puffin Quartet of Poets) and listen to Honegger's "Pacific 231".

Invent your own music that does the same thing. No instruments? Try clapping, or other body sounds.

Pitch

Tunes can go up or down or stay on the same note, which can be high, low, or anywhere in between.

Varying the pitch, highness or lowness of the voice, when reading poetry, can make a radical difference. Try it.

Dynamics

How loud? How quiet? Getting louder? Getting quieter?

Structure

The shape of the whole is determined by using contrast, phrase repetition, different lengths of phrases, pattern variety.

Silence

Don't forget this vital ingredient – before and after and during – for anticipation, surprise and magic.

Using poems with music doesn't mean you have to stick with the words. Use "Jabberwocky" (by Lewis Carroll) to create different atmospheres and feelings. Then use instruments to create similar pictures in sound. Start a collection of poems that can be used in different ways.

It's not what you say, it's the way that you say (play) it!

33

OURSELVES: Voice
An amuse-ical page

The Ha-Ha game
RULE 1. Nobody can laugh
RULE 2. Anyone who does, is sent off by Tom – ref.

★Jasmin starts by shouting a loud 'Ha' to Nyran who is sitting next to her.

★Nyran adds another 'Ha' so turns to Ubaid shouting 'Ha-Ha'.

★Everyone adds a 'Ha' in turn.

★Riaz sees and hears Chander laugh. He sends her to the outside of the circle where she tries to make Nyran laugh by pulling faces and making silly gestures. She must not speak!

★When there are too many Ha's for people to remember, most people are out anyway!

Enjoy it!
Laughter brings smiles, relaxation and a release of natural stimulants into the brain called endorphins. To get them going, tease out that sixth sense we all have – a sense of humour. Forget education. Entertainment is a valuable 'E' factor Be ready with some laughter-starters up your sleeve. The duck-call whistle is a winner – an old song called "The Laughing Policeman" is still on the beat – but don't forget yourself. A funny hat, a wig, or a false nose can help you let your hair down and a surprise 'funny voice' from Mum, Dad and teacher is a sure-fire success.

Vernacular Verses.
Say a sudden 'silly'

A gentleman called to see Mrs Brown
She was having a bath, so wouldn't come down
He said "Slip on something and come down quick"
So she slipped on the soap and was down in a tick!

Body Mix-ups
★Everyone has a piece of paper and pencil.

★Fred asks them to draw a head (with head gear), face and neck at the top of the paper.

★Then Fred asks them to fold over the paper from the top, leaving a bit of neck showing, and pass it to the person on the left.

★The next bit is arms and shoulders to the waist. Fold over to waistline.

★Then waist to ankles and fold over.

★Then feet and footwear and fold over.

★Fred then asks everyone to pass their paper to the left on a rhythmic count, ie Pass and Pass and Pass – and Stop.

★On 'Stop', Fred asks Agnes to open her paper, show it, and guess who did which bit.

Musical Consequences
He: Danny Boy
  met
Her: Daisy
Where: Down at the Old Bull and Bush
He said: "I love you – Yeh Yeh Yeh"
She said: "I'm just wild about Harry"
Consequence was: "Two lovely black eyes"

Daft definitions
Falsetto: Singing through your teeth

PP: Pedal please
FF: Feet first

Funny Bone Songs
Do your ears hang low
Hand knees and boomps-a-daisy
John Brown's baby's got a cold upon its chest
Underneath the spreading chestnut tree
Lambeth Walk
Dem Bones, dem bones, dem dry bones

A bum note
Billy Morgan plays the organ
Sister plays the drum
His Father plays the tambourine
And his mother smacks his Billy Morgan

LAUGHTER THE BEST MEDICINE, Robert Holden, Thorsons

LAUGHTER CLINIC WORKSHOPS, Robert Holden, Tel. 021 551 2932

SILLY AUNT SALLY. Jan Holdstock, Ward Lock Educational

OUR WORLD

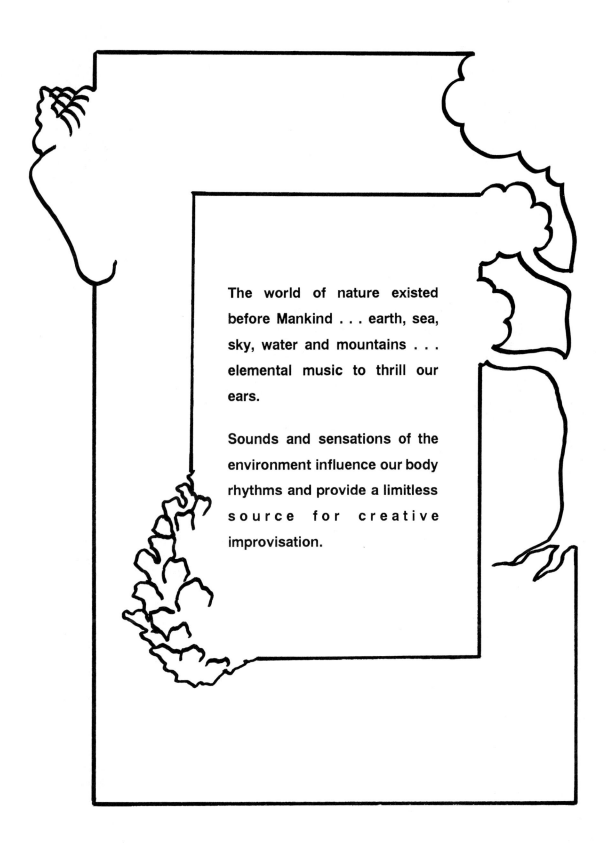

The world of nature existed before Mankind . . . earth, sea, sky, water and mountains . . . elemental music to thrill our ears.

Sounds and sensations of the environment influence our body rhythms and provide a limitless source for creative improvisation.

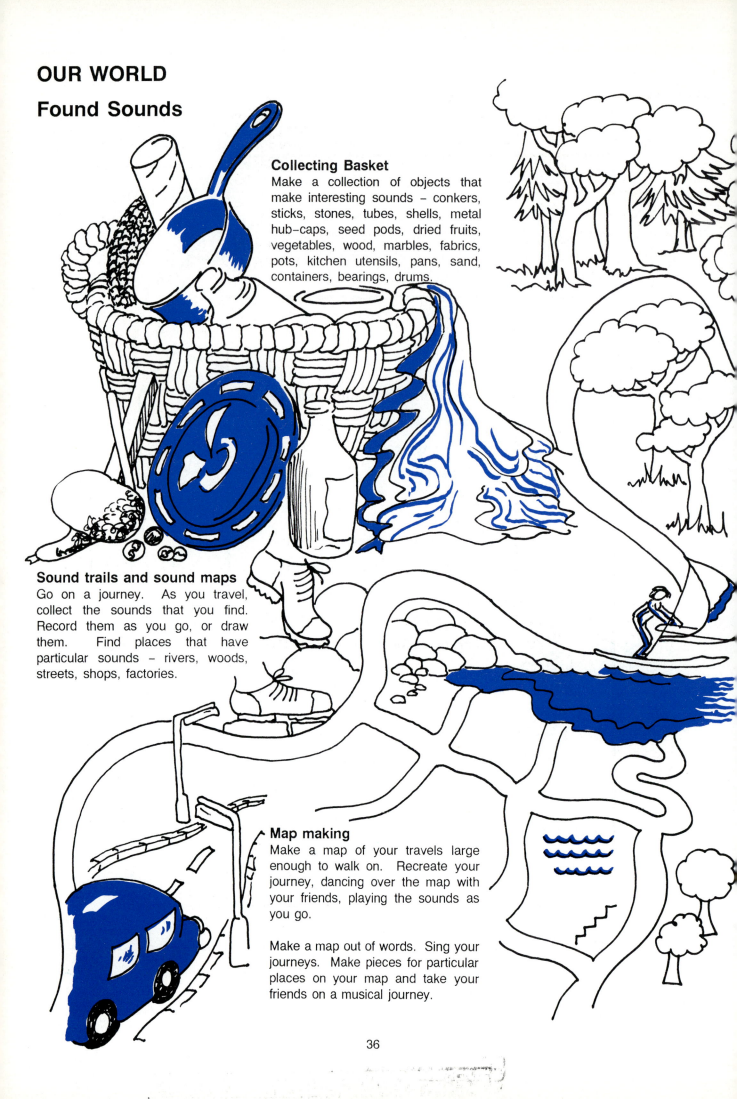

OUR WORLD
Found Sounds

Collecting Basket
Make a collection of objects that make interesting sounds – conkers, sticks, stones, tubes, shells, metal hub–caps, seed pods, dried fruits, vegetables, wood, marbles, fabrics, pots, kitchen utensils, pans, sand, containers, bearings, drums.

Sound trails and sound maps
Go on a journey. As you travel, collect the sounds that you find. Record them as you go, or draw them. Find places that have particular sounds – rivers, woods, streets, shops, factories.

Map making
Make a map of your travels large enough to walk on. Recreate your journey, dancing over the map with your friends, playing the sounds as you go.

Make a map out of words. Sing your journeys. Make pieces for particular places on your map and take your friends on a musical journey.

36

OUR WORLD
Objects for Games and Drama

Paper Orchestra

★Pete devises some visuals to represent sounds that could be made with paper:

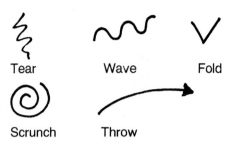

Tear   Wave   Fold

Scrunch   Throw

★Everyone has an old magazine as their instrument and 'plays' as Pete points to the score.

★On the final scrunch, Alice is the first one to make a paper ball and throw it at Pete, so she is the next pointer.

★ New visuals are devised and the score grows.

Confidence Cards

★Everyone sits as an audience, with one chair in solo spot. Each person takes a turn and the rest watch.

★Leader gives Adam a suit of cards. (e.g. Spades, Hearts) He takes one from the deck and looks at it in secret. If the card is a high number Adam is very confident, but if it is a low number, he is extremely shy.

★Adam leaves the room as himself and returns according to the level of confidence shown by his card.

With newspapers invent something to wear. Decide how you can dance in your costume. Can you sing as you go?

★He introduces himself to the audience and they guess which card he drew.

★ Continue the game by setting up short dramatic scenes, eg A policeman with low confidence card and the thief drawing a King. It can become hilarious.

Side-stepping our normal behaviour in playing with card levels, we discover new levels of confidence and acting ability. In the scenes, it is a way of not getting the usual stereotypical stories from situations.

Pass the Parcel ... with a difference.

★Everyone sits or stands in a circle. A balloon, ball or anything to hand is passed round for interest, smell, or tactile stimulation.

★Then pass it again as if it were:
    Hot and likely to burn
    Heavy
    So light it would blow away
    Alive
    A baby

This stimulates the imagination and the senses and gives practice in handling objects with precision.

Tails

★Chris and Bill come out from the group. Chris has a scarf tucked into the back of her trousers. Bill has to steal it without touching Chris.

★Many pairs can now play the game. Make sure you have enough space and the participants do not have any particular spatial disabilities.

A development could be to limit or change the shape of the area. Letting the rest of the group see the strategies and movements, is helpful. It is an excellent ice-breaking game. It develops a strong sense of front and back.

GAMES FOR ACTORS AND NON-ACTORS, Augusta Boal, Routledge

THEATRE GAMES, Clive Barker, Eyre Methuen

OUR WORLD
The Rhythm of Life

Rhythm comes first
We tap toes – feel the beat and want to move – no wonder! We are conceived in rhythm and spend nine months listening to, and feeling regular pulse in a free rhythmic flow of womb–water. In music, pulse develops into the grouping of beats:

> 11　　　(2 time)
> 111　　(3 time)

and free rhythm flows shaped by Mother Nature – a continuance of Life, outside ourselves, of which we are an integral part.

Phrasing
From birth we develop an awareness of how time is phrased:

    beginning and end
    activity and rest
    sound and silence

Phrasing of life is determined by natural events,

    day and night
    light and dark
    tides and seasons

These factors shape and make sense of our lives. Sentences in language are words phrased together to make meaning. Words come from . . .

Pattern
This emerges from a heart beat – BOOM–BA. The first small motif/ pattern which relates to early language, eg Mama, Dada, Hungry, Thirsty. Speech patterning is built on different combinations of strong/weak stresses. In the language of poetry similar stresses form scansion, eg

    iambic   v –
    dactylic   – v v
    anapaestic v v –

This is rhythm
The word derives from the Greek "Rhein" meaning flow. Every culture has its own rhythm, everyone has a personal rhythm. Rhythm orders sound and movement. It is not just keeping time!

The wind doesn't blow in 3/4 time
Rivers don't flow in 6/8 time
And rain doesn't fall in 2/4 time

40

Home Cooking Using Pulses

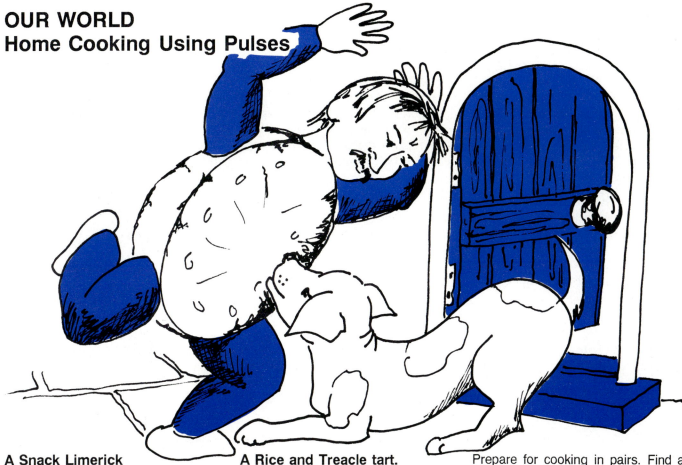

A Snack Limerick

There was a young man of Bengal
Who went to a fancy dress ball
He thought he would risk it
And go as a biscuit
But the dog ate him up in the hall.

★Leader says the limerick in high and low pitched `fun' voices.

★Using thigh strokes and finger clicks, the leader starts up a swingy two pulse for everyone to join in with.

★Leader then says the limerick over the body–pulse.

★All change. Leader does the pulse everyone says the limerick.

★Add instruments and actions to heighten the drama.

★Find word-patterns to say: "fancy dress ball" and "biscuit" mix well. Keep the biscuit crisp! Two short and dry and quick sounds – just as you say it.

★Put these word-patterns on to untuned instruments and you have an accompaniment.

★Why not compose a tune for this limerick?

A Rice and Treacle tart.

Half a pound of tuppeny rice
Half a pound of treacle
That's the way the money goes
`pop' goes the weasel.

Everyone says the jingle and finger taps it on back of hand.

Separate the group. Half say the jingle and the other half choose two body sounds for the pulse –`Trea–cle.

Blend well – then toss ...the groups swop round.

Add colouring. Decide where you can build to a climax or have an echo...

Blend again. Make sure the rhythmic raising agent keeps it light and bouncy.

Divide the `dough' in two and say it as a round.

Ist group
Half a pound of tuppenny rice..
      2nd group
      Half a pound of

Prepare for cooking in pairs. Find a partner and orchestrate the jingle using body percussion and voice. Highlight `pop' with a special sound?

Pot-Boiling Pie.

★Everyone sits in a circle and numbers off starting with Barry at number one, to however many there are.

★Barry starts up a two-pulse and everyone joins in.

★Over this pulse Barry starts the calling chant. He has decided to call Number Three so he says "Number One to Number Three". Without a pause, Number Three picks up the chant and calls someone else e.g. Number nine. "Number three to Number nine". If number nine doesn't keep the pot boiling (missing the pick up) he goes to the end of the circle.
Everyone re-numbers and starts again.

OR: the `dropper' pays a forfeit and it continues without renumbering.
A standing-circle can get a bum-rock/finger click pulse going!

OUR WORLD
More Pulses

Take Five

★Find a recording of music written in five pulse. Dave Brubeck playing "Take Five" on the piano or "Mars Planet Suite", Gustav Holst or 2nd movement of Symphony No 6, Tchaikovsky.

★Starting with thumbs, thrum out a five–pulse on a table top or your knee. Try strong bouncing fingers and smooth joined fingers and light hopping fingers – lots of different qualities to match the character of the music.

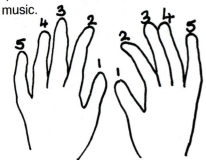

★Find words that scan in five:
Brown as a berry
so is our sherry
It makes us merry
And it is good

★Can you feel the grouping of 3+2 beats?

eg 1 2 3 1 2 | 1 2 3 1 2 ‖

Brown as a berry   so is our sherry

★Say the jingle twice through, adding the 5-finger taps taking care not to add an extra beat on 'good'.

★Find word patterns for ostinato accompaniments – add instruments.

★How about some glass and bottle sounds for flavour?

Rolling and Bouncing

Bouncing the balls on the Lycra trampoline, is a lively and colourful way of making a visual pulse [VN1.8].The group discovers energy and directs it towards their goal.

Rolling the Ball [VN3:10] involved quite complex skills. e.g. hearing a pulse (and a changing one!) translating it into movement and the fine control needed to receive and then roll the ball. It also involved assessing the speed of the ball, its weight, and the surface it was travelling on.

Here are some ways of preparing for this activity.

★Experiment with different sizes and types of ball, offer a choice...Rubber, wool, plastic.

★Consider a variety of `pathways'. For non–ambulant a light–weight plastic  or polystyrene trough could be an excellent `connecting line'.

★Play and sing "Home on the Range" substituting 'action' words for the real ones, ie

and	ROLLing	and	ROLLing and	ROLLing and	ROLLing
oh	give me	a	home – where the	Buff-a-loes	roam ____ keep going

★On the upbeat 'and' the arm prepares with a backward movement for the forward rolling action on the strong beat 'roll'.

★After this rhythmic preparation the real action with the balls can start.

★Before rolling in pairs, devise a game of bowling to sharpen up directional techniques.

★Choose and play music in different pulses always using speech to coordinate rhythmic action eg four–pulse `My Grandfather's Clock'

and	ROLL the	ball and	ROLL the	ball and	ROLL the	ball
my	Grandfather's	clock was too	large for the	shelf so it	stood ninety	years

The Personal Pulse

★This is the most important one. Find the pulse behind your ear lobe. Tune in with your fingers and close your eyes. Start some gentle and rhythmic breathing:

IN two   OUT two   IN two... keep going

then   IN two three   OUT two three

then   to a count of 4 and 5 ... and see how far you can go.

For control, relaxation and a state of wellbeing this activity is the most fundamental of all.

OUR WORLD
Making patterns over pulses

Pendulum Swing

★Make a pendulum by tying a length of string to a stone.

★When the pendulum is set in motion everyone mirrors this pulse with a side-to-side hand movement.

★Sam sings `Speed Bonnie Boat'and everyone joins in adding some body percussion.

★Everyone now wants to make a pendulum using different materials and lengths of string. As many pendulums appear as there are people.

Find out:
Does a heavy `bob' create a slower pace of swing?
What happens when the swing finishes? Does it slow down?

Pendulum Patterns

★Joe makes a visual two-pulse with his arm. It is silent, steady and fairly slow and shaped.

★Using speech sounds, (quiet) untuned percussion and body percussion, everyone in turn, adds a rhythmic pattern, which they go on repeating.

★Joe keeps his pulse going until everyone is playing. He quickens and then slows down the pulse very gradually bringing the composition to silence and stillness.

★This could be notated using words, shapes or pictures.

Here is an example of building word-patterns over a pulse. Start at the bottom of a page and draw Joe's pulse. Keep it widely spaced. The vertical matching must be visual as well as rhythmic!

tidderly tat tiddorly tat

ching – ching ching

tapper tap tapper tap

POM POM POM POM

Responding to a pulse we see can be more difficult than responding to one we hear. Side-to-side hand movements help to absorb the pulse at a physical level.

Songs, rhymes, rap and scat all happening together, over a visual pulse, make exciting textures.

Pendulum play swings into maths and science quite naturally.

Discover that it is only the length of the string which will determine the pace of 'swing'. A pendulum 1 metre long has a beat of 1 second.

Explore clock pendulums, water-dowsing, pocket metronomes.

These ideas are particularly appropriate for the hearing-impaired.

Investigate the giant pendulum in the Science Museum which demonstrates the rotation of the earth on its axis. It is named Foucault's pendulum after its French inventor (Paris 1851).

Pendulum Shapes

Do you remember Max rowing his boat? [VN1.7]. His arc action could start a circle of activities. Consider a possible progression:

★A pendulum swing

inverted becomes an arc

put them together ... a circle

★Let's make these shapes in movement, writing and with our voices.

★Can we see/feel those shapes anywhere?

★Could we use some of these ideas to tell a story about the environment?
  to make bridges?
  to join things together?
  to travel under or over?

and it all started from Max. Thank you.

SOUND INVENTIONS (Book & Video), Richard McNicol, Oxford University Press

OUR WORLD
Transforming the environment

My space

Creating a personal place is very important for everyone ... it happens everywhere ... depending on the space. A shop doorway .. a cardboard house ... a prisoner's cell ... a hospital cubicle ... a room. Imagine the hostage 'in solitary' where the mind has to become the private place ... Remember the refugee and the displaced person who are denied a personal place in the world.

Disorientation in space can be a dilemma... "Where do I go?" ... "Where do I sit?"... "I need a nest".

★Make a bum seat. Trace round curves and make a paper pattern.

★The shape can be marked on a floor with coloured tape, or more permanently, make a portable 'bumpetty pad' out of foam, carpet or cushion.

★Add a mark or name, personally made if possible.

There are many games to play if everyone has a bumpetty pad or a chair to sit on.

Changing places

★"I'll change places with Romayne" says Aneesa.
Romayne is glad Aneesa chose him ... he likes her.

★"I'll change places with Darlene" says Jenna.
Jenna enjoys dancing across the space and says "Hi" to Darlene in her wheel chair as they pass.

★"I'll change places with Hilda" says Harry. He's glad to get off his chair and move to a new place in the room. "Sometimes" says Harry "Molly plays music when we move... She played some shuffling sounds with her hands as I changed places with Hilda"

★"Then Molly started taking chairs away and we had to find one to sit on quickly. Occasionally we get prizes; I won a china dog which I keep on my locker".

Changing things ...

lighting
temperature
colour
sound
sight
smell
comfort

★Someone wanting to change places with you is a special way of being chosen.

★It adds to the fun, to greet the person you are changing places with, as you pass.

★A gentle accompaniment can support or initiate, the way people move across the space.

★Excitement and mobility are increased when chairs are taken away.

★With extra pairs of hands 'touch pathways', using Thera-band or long pieces of material, can develop ability of 'feeling' where you're going.

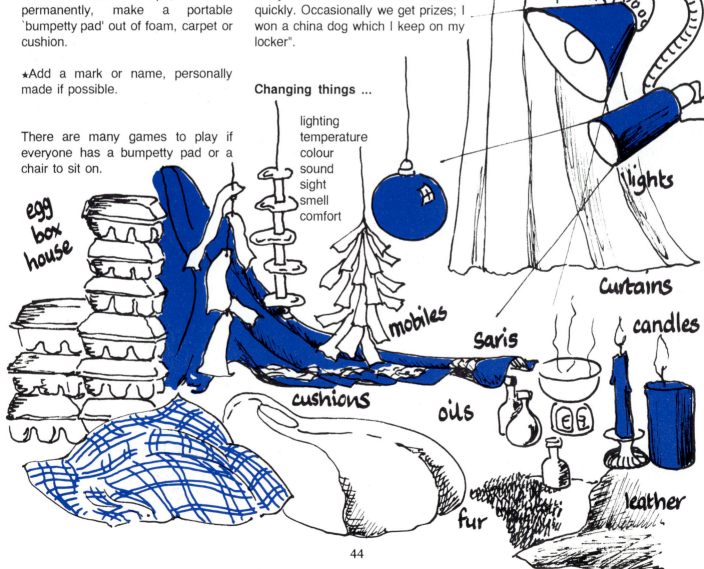

egg box house

cushions

mobiles

saris

oils

fur

lights

curtains

candles

leather

Our Jungle at Rimnicu Sarat

Every person alive has an imagination. Those with special needs or poor life experience, require greater encouragement and stimulation to trigger the imagination.

Creating an environment can be a total experience of investigative learning, participation and decision making and finally, the unforgettable magic of another world.

From the beginning, involvement is essential. Watching something grow is an invaluable process. Self–discipline develops within this less formal structure and successful behaviour modification can also be achieved. Music, Dance, Drama and making things, all come together . . . no bar lines or divisions

What to do

★Introduce the children to the jungle to be at the beginning. Describe the project so that they can `see' it for themselves.

★Make foot and hand prints on the lined walls for foliage and tree trunks.

★Construct large animals with ears and trunks for hiding in and underneath.

★Put lining paper on walls and lower the ceiling with combat net for dangling vines, animals, birds, to touch and blow and look at.

★Hang yellow and green cellophane in loose strips over windows to give eerie moving light.

★Camouflage cupboards with paper or material. Put up animal pictures covered with strips of foil and cellophane for children to `discover' the pictures. If you have a pyramid this becomes a den for the animals.

★End each session with quiet time and relaxation. Weave a story. Include children by name. Talk about the animals and introduce role play. Emphasise the joy of friendship, trust and sharing.

★End each story time with a beginning of what's to come ...

Creating magic

An overhead projector can 'springboard' art activities, pictures in sound, animating stories ... reminiscence work.
Using coloured acetate, doilies and cut paper, can change a group's mood by relaxing or stimulating.
Moving patterns can be made by dripping paint and oil into water with a little washing/up liquid or encapsulating them into transparencies.

Remember: Aromatherapy, Massage, Shiatsu, Guided Fantasy.

bar chimes

rakatak

rain maker

pyramid

OUR WORLD
Electronic Magic

Modulating natural sounds

Look at and listen to the compositions that the groups made from environmental sounds [VN2.1] and read about plate mics and echo machines. This new dimension of transforming the sounds they had created, through electronic means, was an exciting experience for the children. Experimentation was unending: "What did it sound like? How can we change it? What happens if...?" Questions which did not have right and wrong answers, gave rise to decision–making, based on "Does that sound OK"?... if not – why not?" Truly the stuff of composition. Recording the compositions also gave them a sound base for movement creativity.

Starting off

So an inexpensive mic and amplifier is a basic first piece of equipment. A way of `sounding-out' that can open up voices, enrich small voices, and become a passport to every sort of music–making. Investigate prices and possibilities of a plate mic and an echo machine.

Finding out

There is another small, easily made and inexpensive piece of equipment called a Transducer.

Come on a journey that will take you into a magic scene of secret sounds.

First we need to collect some electronic equipment together – hang on, don't go! What we need is readily available and very inexpensive. An electronic amplifier is needed, and you are likely to be spoiled for choice. Record players, cassette recorders, music centres and radios all contain an electronic amplifier which can be used for this work. Look on the equipment for input sockets which are usually labelled:– Microphone, CD, Aux, Tape, Radio, Tuner, cartridge, phono, or DAT. You may have an amplifier you use with a microphone or electronic instrument already, so to use that would be straightforward.

The electronic ear we are going to use is called a "Piezo Transducer". The transducer is a wafer thin disc about 2cm in diameter and has two short wires attached to it. The wires need to be wrapped round the transducer. Use clear tape to hold them in place and to stop them pulling away. Increase the length of the two wires on the transducer by adding a long length of 2 core wire. Add an audio plug onto the end of the wire suitable to fit the input socket on your amplifier. Do not allow the two wires to touch at the join or in the audio plug. Put insulation tape on the joins. (see diagram).

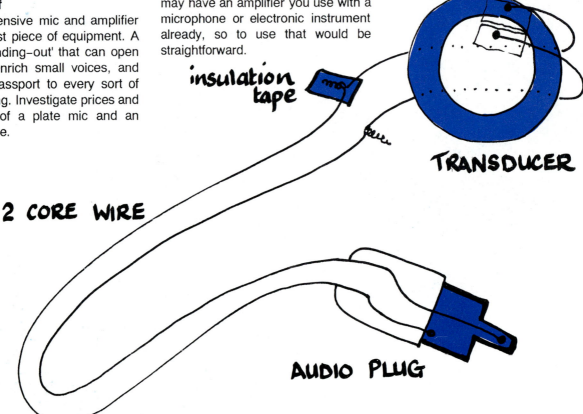

insulation tape

TRANSDUCER

2 CORE WIRE

AUDIO PLUG

PIEZO TRANSDUCERS (approx 30p) and SMALL BATTERY AMPLIFIERS (approx £15.00), MPS, PO Box 777, Rayleigh, Essex SS6 8LU, Tel. 0702 552961

CREATIVE APPROACHES TO NEW TECHNOLOGY, Workshops, Collaborations, Studio Design, Sonic Arts Network, Tel. 043 835 9344

MIDI CREATOR by DAWSONS, Tel. 0925 32591

Plug the transducer in and turn the amplifier on. Gradually bring up the volume until you can hear the transducer being moved in your hand. Move the transducer away from the speaker if you get a feed-back "howl". Hold the transducer against a rubber band, a shoe lace, a long piece of string, or a hair and then pluck away. Use a piece of "Blu-Tack" to stick the transducer to a clockwork clock, a hand whisk, a door hinge. Listen to Sellotape, cutting with scissors, swallowing, the vocal cords, the list is endless. There are some good sounds to be made with water but only use a battery powered amplifier for wet work. Avoid very old amplifiers which use valves. Ask someone if you are unsure about electrical connections.

A Harmonizer
This equipment can change the pitch of a sound played or turn one voice into a choir or a monster!

A Reverberation machine
Consider this equipment which will turn your room into a cave or a cathedral.

If you aren't switched on yet, then try this EAR GONG for private music
You need..... I person
1 coathanger
2 pieces of string
about 60 cm long

Make a loop in the string. Then put your fingers through the loops and put them in your ears. Let the coathanger dangle. Knock it against things what does it sound like? How can you play this music to other people? How can you use the ear-gong as a listening device?

Make sure that all equipment is safe and checked.

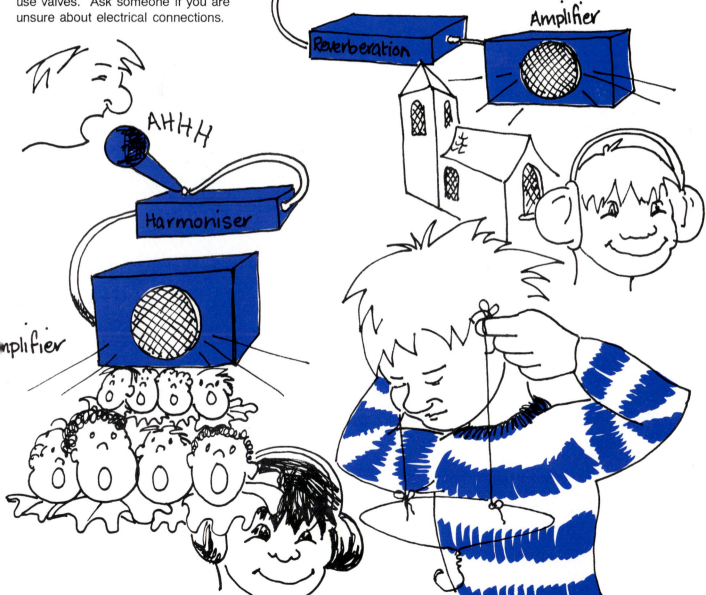

DESIGNING SOUND (Book & Software), Phil Ellis, Tel. 0608 811488

E.M.S. SOUNDBEAM, Tim Swingler, Tel. 0603 631647

OUR WORLD
Circle the Earth with Dance

"Dance dance . . ."
Movement in a garden, twirling ribbons, a steam engine; the video shows a wealth of ideas you may like to develop.

Dance into winter
Could you 'grow' this from "Take two feet?" (page 8).

★How do we move on frosty surfaces? In snow and slush?

★Contrast freeze (outside) with thaw (inside).

★Does the clothing we wear affect the way we walk?

A range of shapes
Everyone in the circle holds a piece of Lycra by the edges, down to the floor. Mel and Zaquia go underneath. Pushing upwards into the material with fingers, toes, elbows etc they make peaks and folds. Find some music and make a dance – of movement and stillness.

Starting from the music
Choreograph a rainforest dance from the music [VN2.9]. How could the sounds be interpreted in movement? Would the calypso sections beginning and end contrast with the middle section – if so, how? Can you improvise some props? Or costumes?

A movement sculpture with colour
Hold lengths of coloured Lycra or Thera-band between pairs and explore waving, stretching, see-saws and weaving. Using one or two ideas only, create a simple dance, with or without music. For a finale, each person in turn moves underneath the material, and around a person, until a sculpture in stillness evolves.

Be "Quickness and Lightness"
Take on the quality. Don't just imitate. Look at the Aquarium [VN2.6] and develop the movement ideas by exploring different levels. Look at the fishes darting, hiding gliding. Explore those qualities. Can the musicians find unconventional sounds? Fingers and brushes and beads dangled over tuned percussion? Watery mouth and tongue sounds?

Old Thyme
Ask the over-sixties family and friends to dance and tell you about:
   Conga
   Palais Glide
   Lambeth Walk
   Hands Knees and Boomps-a-daisy

Circle dance
Make your own to the tune "Yellow Bird". Repeated phrases to a count of eight, form the structure of the music. (This traditional eight-bar measure underlies much folk, country, square and old time dance).

Decide
★How you move, ie walk, skip, gallop, individually, in pairs.

★Where you move, ie around or in and out of a circle or a square.

★What levels, ie rising and falling – high medium or low, gathering and scattering.

★Try out ideas on your own and then make a dance plan
●introduction
●moves and rests
●finish

★Note the tape-counter numbers at phrase beginnings and write them in on your dance plan. They are needed for rehearsal.
OR
Find a technical assistant.

I came, I saw, I conga'd!!!

How about
●*composing a Whirlie water-ballet to Tchaikovsky's "Waltz of the Flowers" (Nutcracker Suite)*
●*starting a 'movement' choir. Created by Rudolf Laban (the founder of Modern Educational Dance) a 'movement' choir can be very exciting.*
"It was an unforgettable experience dancing to the final chorus of Bach's St Matthew Passion" . . . a 25-year old.

THERA-BAND (stretch material), Nottingham Rehab, 17 Ludlow Hill Road, West Bridgford, Nottingham

DANCING CIRCLES (Books) PO 26, Glastonbury, Somerset BA6 9YA

OUR INSTRUMENTS

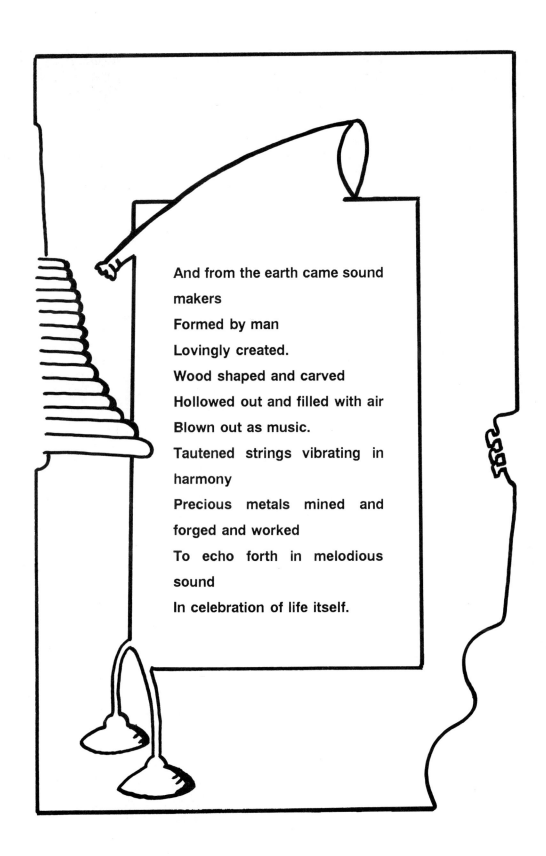

And from the earth came sound makers
Formed by man
Lovingly created.
Wood shaped and carved
Hollowed out and filled with air
Blown out as music.
Tautened strings vibrating in harmony
Precious metals mined and forged and worked
To echo forth in melodious sound
In celebration of life itself.

OUR INSTRUMENTS
The Shaker Family

Rattlin' Rockin' Rollin'
As human beings we move but we don't make sounds, unless we are wearing baubles, bangles and beads or our bones have skeletonized and our teeth rattle.

A profound thought but one with some interesting implications. If bodies don't move, muscles atrophy. If minds are not stimulated, stagnation and deprivation follow. Everyone needs to shake. Yet unaided the shaking human body makes no sound.

To move and dance
The bouncing baby is healthy, because it moves, and is moved up and down.

Rock 'n Roll in the Fifties was exciting because it made us want to dance – we did – and felt better for doing so. Think of the stimulating feeling of Latin American dance and the proven popularity of the Hokey Cokey.

When asked to tap the paper tambourines [VN3.7], some of the children shake them. This basic movement response (up and down) is easier than repeated movement i.e. tapping.

Alison chose to vocalise and move her finger on the zig-zag pattern. Follow her score to find your sound and movement responses to the different designs [VNI.5]. The sign for tremolo (a shaking sound) in music is

enlarge it and you have a "wave"

A child's goodbye follows the same movement pattern. So does a Hello handshake. Are there connections here?

We need a 'shaker'
When you provide a wide selection of sound-makers, it is noticeable how many choose shakers. This would seem to support the need we all have to shake. For those who are physically disadvantaged, being able to shake a sound can compensate for inability to make a movement. Tailor-made shakers are essential in special care; a poppy-seed-head can stimulate an eyelid flicker response.

For many babies a rattle is a first instrument; a shaker is often the first instrument we make. The last sound we make is, in some civilisations, marked by the playing of a rattle – the death rattle.

. . . Which says it all
The word links reflect this closeness of movement and sound set up by shaking.

Look at the instrument illustrations. Say their names, out loud, and pretend to play the instruments AT THE SAME TIME, tossing the pattern from hand to hand – maracas, cabasas.

Notice the names are all multi-syllabic, ie more than ONE movement and sound is needed to make a shake.

Does a bell ring when you say "tintinnabulate"?

Will you believe that "shoggle" is in the dictionary and means wobble rock? And that the definition of a football rattle is "a mechanical stridulator"?

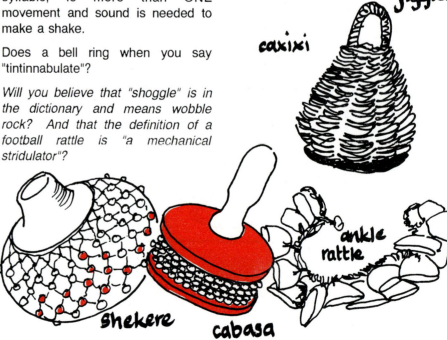

tinkler bell

dandiya

Ting a ling chimes

wire woggler

halo jiggler

caxixi

chocolo

shekere

cabasa

ankle rattle

50

Make and Shake a Jingle Ring
Tune: In and out the windows

Sitting in a circle
Sitting in a circle
Sitting in a circle
We'll make the Jingle Ring

Chorus
Jingle Ringle Tingle
Jingle Ringle Tingle
Jingle Ringle Tingle
Making shaky sounds.

Lift up very slowly
Lift up very slowly
Lift up very slowly
And down it comes again.

Chorus

Neema shakes a solo
Neema shakes a solo
Neema shakes a solo
Listen while she plays.

Pass the ring around
Pass the ring around
Pass the ring around
And find a different sound.

Chorus

Jingle Ring is tired
Jingle Ring is tired
Jingle Ring is tired
It's going to have a rest.

Making connections
A circle is always magical – a 'shaking' circle even more so. A plastic hoop gives a firm circle structure and connects people in a more tangible way than the Whirlie Ring [VN1.6]. It also gives practice in function grasp hold and release for those with cerebral palsy.

In addition to ideas for directional movement, included above, the jingle ring has unlimited potential.

★Collecting. Making things to hang on the hoop, eg keys, bells, beads, wooden balls, ie anything of colour, perfumed or tactile interest.

★Creating visual sequences to play.

★Guessing games. "What am I touching?" leading to story telling.

A sequence to play

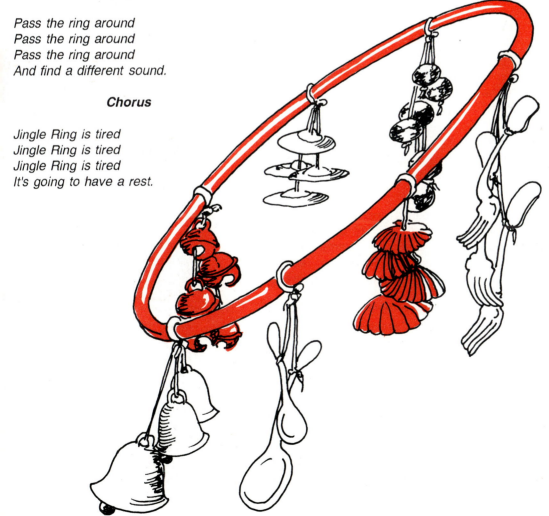

OUR INSTRUMENTS
The Shaker Family

The Shaking Snake
Shaking sounds and movements can, on the one hand be stimulating, as we see in the story that follows, or, on the other, be relaxing and soothing, as the section "The Dreamland Tree" explains.

"A kind but very lonely snake called Shikarolla lived in a field near a big house far away from a town. Many children lived in the house; some of their names were Maria, Ovidiu, Ionut.

Their dark eyes looked sad and their ears never heard Shikarolla. He was a shy snake and swished his way quietly through the long grass.

Shikarolla was always cold and hungry – poor Shikarolla. One day he heard some exciting sounds so he slithered towards the big house and sat listening outside the window to the music.

Shikarolla loved the sounds – they made him feel different. He began to move up and down; suddenly he found he was shaking with laughter."

This story was one way the Romanian children expressed their feelings through shakers ... all sizes, shapes and sound qualities.

Awakening this response was a stimulating experience for everyone. Belief in the power of music and dance and the magic of a story to affect human behaviour was renewed.

★Seeing the children's joy in their first exploration of storytelling through musical images, was an unforgettable experience.

★Stories tailor-made to circumstances, are always winners and can become a vehicle for whatever sounds and movements you wish to introduce.

★Over-stimulation through shaking activities can result in a group becoming high and over-excited. Bring the session to a close with a calming activity ... some quiet music or a peaceful painting activity.

Paper Snakes
Simple Origami of folding paper.

Icing Sugar Snakes
Paint paper with a solution of icing sugar and water. Drip thin paint snake shapes onto paper and leave to dry over night. When dry they will be shiny.

Snake Posture. Sarpasana. Try this yoga exercise to help your breathing.

The Dreamland Tree
*"Mother shakes the dreamland tree
Down falls a little dream for thee"*

The tradition of rocking children to sleep and singing lullabies, although not in common practice today, has links with the Shaker family.

The person who needs calming has 'inner commotion', ie shaking inside. To communicate with that feeling, we use a physical movement, ie rocking; treating like with like overcomes the agitation within.

Similarly with behavioural disturbance. Instead of offering quiet, calm activities, we can scream with the screamer, stamp with the stamper. The person recognizes his/her movements are being copied. This conscious recognition of 'something different happening' can be the beginning of contact for structuring new strategies, eg start/stop – me/you . . . This technique of "going along with" can be the first step in breaking stereotypical behaviour.

It is called the iso-principle (isos = the same, Gk) and can be compared to homeopathy, eg by administering the same substance of that which causes the illness, like cures like.

Other starters for stories:
The rattle snake who lost his rattle
The Medicine Man

Veronica Sherborne, author of "Developmental Movement for Young Children" quoted the young adult with severe behavioural problems who needed a swing before the session.

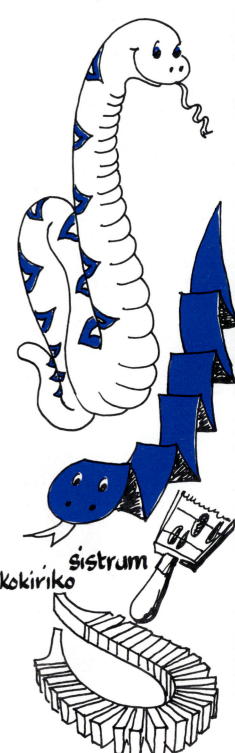

sistrum

Kokiriko

MUSIC THERAPY and the AUTISTIC CHILD, Alvin & Warwick, Oxford University Press
KEY CONCEPTS IN THE ORFF MUSIC THERAPY, Gertrud Orff, Schott

Spotlight on Shakers

★Everyone chooses an instrument from a selection of scrapers, tappers, shakers, blowers, pluckers.

★Leader uses body movements to stimulate a sound. Recall VN1.3 – Ian moved and his orchestra played only if they had a sound which matched his movement. If Ian was still they were silent.

★Leader asks everyone to group into families. (The striking–tapping family will find they play on a variety of surfaces e.g. wood, skin, metal bone, glass – the tambourine players will find they belong to the shaking and tapping families).

★Talk about the differences and similarities of the instruments. Explain that some instruments are tuned to a 'definite' pitch.

★Now repeat the conducting activity and contrast the different qualities that emerge.

★Each group (except the shakers) then works on a simple compositional idea ... aiming for a firm beginning and ending.

★The shakers devise a processional idea. They visit the other groups in turn and invite them to share their composition.

Make clear movements. Experiment with arm, head and finger wiggles, weighty punches. Keep eye contact with your orchestra. Look at, and listen to their responses. They are discovering different ways of playing one sound–maker, concentrating on looking AND making decisions – so proceed slowly from one idea to the next.

The interrelated qualities of movement and sound are:

Weight: strong and fine tension
DYNAMICS: Loud – Quiet

Levels: (Different planes)
PITCH: High – Low

Sustained and broken flow
DURATION: Long – Short

Speed: (Fast and slow)
PACE: Fast – Slow

Focus on pair work – one mover and one musician, to let them experience these linked qualities. Simple shapes of form and phrasing will begin to emerge ... show them and share them.

Point out the skills of:

★*Making continuous sound on percussion i.e. alternate "sticking" with two beaters – LRLRLRLRLRLR.*

★*Damping metal instruments*

★*Understanding that the up and down (vertical) signal of pitch ↕ needs a 'physical' transition to left and right ↔ (horizontal) when playing keyboards and tuned percussion.*

The ideas on this page are developmental and could extend over a period of time, using classroom and hall space. Working towards a performance can highlight efforts made and achieve a sense of theatre.

DEVELOPMENTAL MOVEMENT for CHILDREN, Veronica Sherborne, Cambridge University Press
VERONICA SHERBORNE WORKSHOPS, Cyndi Hill, Tel. 0272 373647

OUR INSTRUMENTS
Whirlie Bandemonium

There are some sound-makers in the 'toy' category that can be great additions to one's instrumentarium. The whirlie is one of them. In its own right it becomes a musical instrument.

The video shows some ways of using whirlies, but this section, in cartoon style, further illustrates its potential as a serious as well as a fun instrument.

Tune: "O My little Augustin" or "Don't put your muck in our dustbin".

We all want a whirlie, a whirlie, a whirlie,
It is long and curly and makes lots of sounds,
Tap, twist and shake it ... then
Twirl – a – sound and scrape it
We all want a whirlie, they're good fun to play!

★Twirl a whirlie very slowly and listen for the low tone it will make. Tune into that sound with your humming voice.

★Then twirl a little faster for the next tone ... going up... and getting faster ... until you make the highest one. You should be able to hear three and maybe four tones.

★Blow over the top of the tube and tap it on the floor and you will hear that first tone you started with.

From the length and diameter of the tube and material used (in this instance, plastic), one basic tone is produced. This is called the Fundamental ... the tones above it are called overtones. This harmonic series is pure science and is the foundation of all pitched instruments. (Elementary acoustics are worth investigating).

WHIRLIES, Available PO Box 149, NG3 5PU

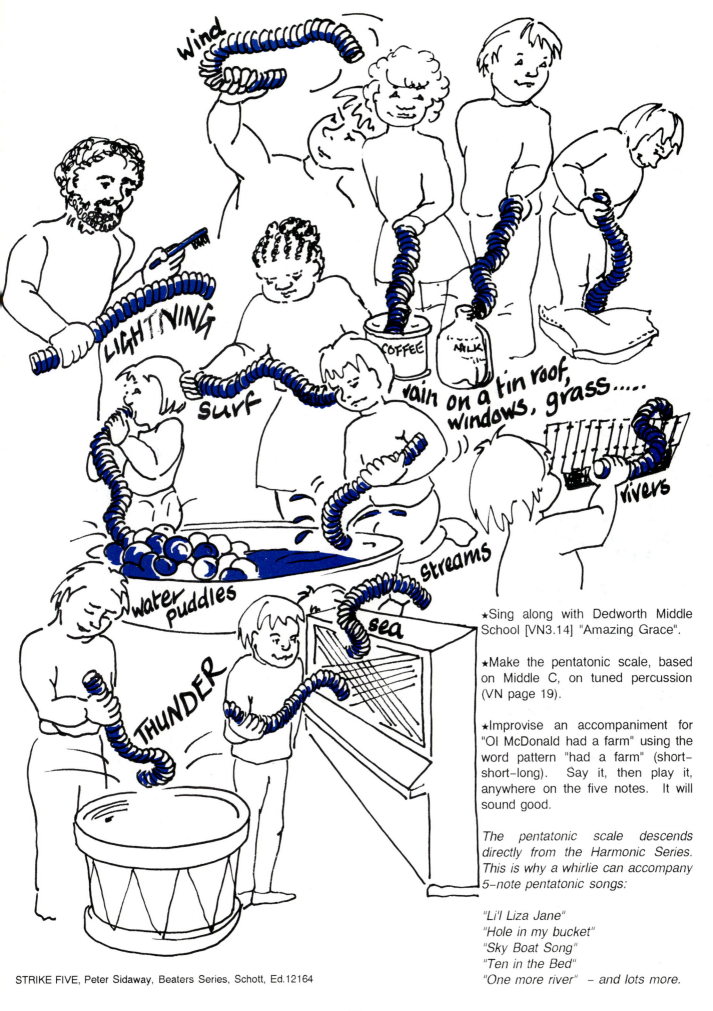

Labels within the illustration: wind, LIGHTNING, surf, rain on a tin roof, windows, grass....., water puddles, streams, rivers, sea, THUNDER, COFFEE, MILK

★Sing along with Dedworth Middle School [VN3.14] "Amazing Grace".

★Make the pentatonic scale, based on Middle C, on tuned percussion (VN page 19).

★Improvise an accompaniment for "Ol McDonald had a farm" using the word pattern "had a farm" (short-short-long). Say it, then play it, anywhere on the five notes. It will sound good.

The pentatonic scale descends directly from the Harmonic Series. This is why a whirlie can accompany 5-note pentatonic songs:

"Li'l Liza Jane"
"Hole in my bucket"
"Sky Boat Song"
"Ten in the Bed"
"One more river" – and lots more.

STRIKE FIVE, Peter Sidaway, Beaters Series, Schott, Ed.12164

55

OUR INSTRUMENTS
Musical Games

Crocodile bites

★Everyone chooses an instrument and sits or stands in a circle.

★Duncan establishes a clear visual signal that means stop.

★Hold your hands together like a crocodile's mouth

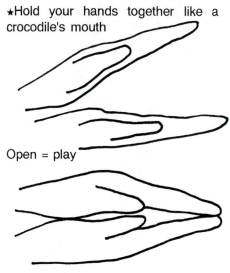

Open = play

Closed = stop

★Duncan invites everyone to play – any sound they like at any volume. The catch is that if someone plays when the crocodile's mouth is shut or doesn't play at all, they are out and become the crocodile. Chandra is crocodile no 2 and continues the game.

★Duncan becomes a watcher to help Chandra spot those going out. Continue until there is a winner.

It's Bill. Everyone applauds.

★Bill chooses a cymbal and asks the group to close their eyes and move a hand for as long as they hear the sound. When the cymbal sound stops, everyone is still.

Bill plays the cymbal for each one in turn. In the silences they sing or play an instrument – a solo spot. The cymbal is now a 'stop' signal and everyone can be in the control role and choose how and when to play. All change instruments and start again.

Let's make a sandwich

A   We all do something together. Collective affirmation.

B   Someone does something alone. Breaking out.

A   We all do something together back in a group.

Some experience of a mixture of sound ingredients (conventional and unconventional) is needed before starting this activity.

Choosing what to play is as important as playing.

Understanding that loud and vigorous exploration of sound-makers is natural.

Let it happen!

Taking turns in controlling the group sound is good; the player who goes out, comes in as the crocodile.

It is important that people who are not used to playing instruments have a chance to really have a go, even if this means ten minutes of chaos.

What did that sound like?
How would we change it next time?
Could you hear everyone?
What did it make you feel like?
When we start again, shall we all start together or one at a time?

Asking questions that focus on listening and decision-making skills is helpful.

Making a gentle movement as you listen helps concentration. It also gives visual feedback to the leader.

Focusing on a sound that decays into silence, we hear the environmental sounds around us.

Spotlighting a player in the 'jam' role – B – is like 'taking a break' in jazz.

These beginnings of composition and decision-making are important for the group and the individual.

MUSIC STARTERS, Orff Society (UK), 31 Roedean Crescent, London SW15 5JX

Chance and choice

"Lets play a game – Once Upon a time"

"We're going to have a Treasure Hunt"

However young we are, games of chance, surprises, and excitement always bewitch and fascinate. Lots of games need a person to start. Here are some ideas.

★Hide a sweet. Whoever finds the sweet is the starter person.

★The first person who can bring a leaf is the starter person.

★Hand out pieces of paper with lucky numbers or secret messages on.

★One potato, two potato – a jingle where pointing produces the starter person.

Lucky Dip

★Fill a box with a mixture of sound makers.

★Leader asks five people to have a lucky dip.

★Leader says "Play your instrument and imagine who or what you would like to be from the sound" (suggestions may help).

★After thinking time, each person in turn plays and says "I'd like to be –".

★The listening group are then asked "What is Jola going to be?"

★Leader then weaves a wonderful story bringing in the characters who then respond in sound. The listening group support with weather sounds, laughter, applause – on cue.

Pre-selecting sounds ensures variety. A very withdrawn child can use a security toy; add a bell to give it a voice.

By starting from sound, the imagination can be fired into a world of fantasy. Each offering of the group, recalled in turn, will be a memory aid to the leader.

Role play through instruments can release a range of feelings. With sensitive handling this activity can ease trauma or be a vehicle for laughter and learning. The role of the story teller is a responsible one. Don't break the tension!

Throw the dice

★Find the first dice thrower – it's Danuta.
★Danuta throws the dice and calls out somebody's name – it's Jattin.
★Jattin reads that four is the number on top of the dice so he starts a four pulse with body sounds. Everyone joins in with Jattin.
★When the group has got going, Jattin then sings or chooses an instrument to improvise over the four pulse.
★Jattin throws the dice and the game continues.

SOUND WAVES, Leonora Davies, Unwin Hyman

OUR INSTRUMENTS
Some jazzy cookin'

Rock buns
Ingredients:

★Current personnel using body percussion and voice.
★A portion of crisp, dry words
★A handful of skins
★A spoonful of cymbals (imitated and played)
★Four measures of rhythm
★Some dashes of dance routine
★A pound of black bin-liners to wear.

Mix gradually and to taste.
Feeling a steady four-pulse start up:

	Bum Rock /	Finger Click /	Bum Rock /	Finger Click – keep going
Add words	ROCK	two	three	four
	ROCK	two	three	we're gonna
	ROCK	two	three	and
	Keep	it	cool	
Add skins	Boom	(nod)	boom	(nod)
Add cymbal	(nod)	P'teesh't	(nod)	P'teesh't

Add a pinch of ... "Be-doo-dah" – "chickety wah".
Throw in a (l)egg or two ... Bring on the dancers.
Divide the mixture – Make a separate rhythm group.

Take a break ... Stir in the solo spots.

`Put on the style' and a recording of Rock Music if you need support.

HAVE FUN
There is nothing like a dance routine to create fun time for all ages. Sometimes a small volunteer group will go off with a few ideas, and return to galvanize the rest into a song and dance act.

OR – a tap dancer or high-kicking stepper may be in the wings, awaiting discovery. Providing props and costumes will help disperse embarrassment. Remember the hats and dark glasses? [VN3.15]

JAZZYLOPHONE, Kate Baxter (Beaters Series), Schotts, Ed 12168

OUR INSTRUMENTS
Blowing off steam

Sound ways of working

All of us feel angry at times for a variety of reasons. Accepting the fact may be difficult, expressing feelings of anger even more so. Some of us hit out, some of us withdraw. By using the earth as a sounding board through stamping, and using instruments as extensions of our voice, this helps us to externalize our inner feelings. Group chanting can be a way of letting this happen. Here are some ideas you may like to talk about and try with your groups.

Sometimes a song, poem, or event in life can open a door into talking about our feelings and getting in touch with them. It may help to write these down and share them later in pairs or with the group.

Find some feelings that may be common to everybody – or nearly. "I feel silly, people laugh at me". "I get angry because nobody understands"

Talk about issues – encourage pair discussion. With permission from the group, write down findings and shape them in some way. eg Why do I get angry? Are the reasons within me? (physical pain) or external? Can I control them if I have some options to make change? Are they beyond my control?

If the group are willing to 'sound out' their feelings, talk about possible words for a spoken chant. Keep it short – "We are angry" could be enough. Repeat it getting louder and louder and finishing with a cymbal crash. Add foot and hand stamps on the floor if possible.

Having set the chant, suggest that small groups work separately. Encourage more speak-out or scream-out, in pairs or individuals, on anything they want to say.

If appropriate, talk with the groups, supporting and accepting their ideas, with no criticism. They may like to share ideas. If so make a sequence of group contributions, sandwiching them between the chant.
eg Chant – Group 1 contribution – Chant – Group 2 contribution. Find a way of winding down gently; when words are not easy to find a group hug can say everything.

LEARNING TOGETHER, Video/Book Pack, Dan Hobbs, Hexagon Publishing Ltd, 5 Vickerage Lane, New Malden, Surrey KT3 3RZ
ONCE UPON A GROUP, Michael Kindred, 20 Dover Street, Southwell, Notts NG25 0EZ

OUR INSTRUMENTS
Playing accompaniments

Getting started

Singing is an important activity in which to involve your group. It is fundamental to language development, with songs providing a precise framework, pinpointing words, shaping phrases and involving voice modulation.

"Can we sing that song again?" says everything about the need to sing and express ourselves through a lyric and our voice. Playing a simple accompaniment on a guitar, chromaharp, omnichord, tuned percussion and keyboard, opens up a whole new world of musical achievement.

Chordal instruments

The chromaharp, as you hear and see on the video, sounds good and is easy to play. The chord bars, felted underneath, select the strings needed in each chord by a system of damping; all you have to do is find the appropriate chord, firmly press the white button, and strum with the other hand.
Hey Presto!
An omnichord is an electronic version of the Chromaharp and has exceptional playing potential for people with severe disabilities. With a touch sensitive panel, the lightest movement of finger, tongue or toe, will give an exciting sound reward.

But time for a little fantasy: Imagine a performer at a folk evening or a guitar vocalist. They are using the skills that are required for playing an effective accompaniment with our group.

Look at the skills they are using:
● They are taking the lead by singing out with confidence.
● They know the song they are singing in their heads.
● They are using an instrument to play chords to complement their singing.
● They give the appearance of it being natural and easy for them. In reality they have prepared and

practised before going public.

Playing an accompaniment need not involve playing the tune. The three basic requirements are knowing what chords to play, when, and where to find them on an instrument.

Take a well known tune...Happy Birthday...You can see that there are only three chords to play, so it requires you to be familiar with these chords (GC and D7) on the instrument you play. (They are adjacent on the Chromaharp and Omnichord).

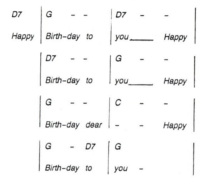

D7	G – –	D7 – –
Happy	Birth-day to	you____ Happy
	D7 – –	G – –
	Birth-day to	you____ Happy
	G – –	C – –
	Birth-day dear	– – Happy
	G – D7	G
	Birth-day to	you –

Find the chord bars and play them slowly in sequence. Then say the words and match them with the chords. Work slowly in these early stages and always with a strong rhythmic feeling of pulse. Add a three–pulse strum, stroking the strings through bass to treble. Tune in with your voice and you are making music. Which hand you use depends on whether you are right or left handed. Alison uses a right handed strum crossing over her left hand on the chord buttons. [VN1.10]. There is no right or wrong way; just suitability for you.

Play and sing along with Alison in "Stroke, stroke, stroke your legs" (to the tune of "Row Row Row your Boat") [VN1.10]. It uses only one chord – C major, or choose your own.

The key of B♭ major is comfortable and very accessible on chromaharps; it is particularly suited, as a singing key, to groups with special needs.

A word about TUNING. With a chromatic electronic tuner, it is no longer a problem. This reasonably priced piece of equipment gives maximum accuracy and minimum hassle!

omnichord.

OMNICHORDS (all models) from KES Music Services, 26 Elms Road, Harrow, Middlesex HA3 6BQ

STROKES and STRUMS for the AUTOHARP and CHROMAHARP, Tim Gauntley, PO Box 149, NG3 5PU

Recommended models are 21 bar instruments (see below for stockists). With this chord power, you will be able to play from a wide range of song books. Making your own word song sheets (as in Happy Birthday) gives you a personal repertoire. Write down the words on card that will fit in a card index box, with chord names written accurately over words and in a bright colour.

Word song sheets, eg Community Songs, Nursery Rhymes and Songs and Christmas Carols are referenced below together with tutors. These starter supports may encourage you to play a chromaharp: once you have started you will want to continue.

Tuned percussion
The preparation is now done for adding chime–bars, xylophones and glockenspiels to play `single note' accompaniments using the same sequence, ie the letter name of the chord will correspond with the same letter name on all the tuned percussion. So with two beaters play this single note accompaniment.

D	G G G	D D D
Happy	Birth–day to	you___ Happy

D D D	G G G
Birth–day to	you___ Happy

G G G	C C C
Birth–day dear	– – Happy

G G D	G –
Birth–day to	you –

When the pulse is secure, start improvising rhythmic patterns. A mixture of both makes a weave accompaniment.

Electronic Keyboard (auto–chord system)
With keyboards, most of them have an automatic chord playing function. As the player uses one finger a keyboard will play a full accompaniment simulating more than one instrument playing, all based round the one note pressed. To play "Happy Birthday" you will need to find a waltz style. After finding the style you also need to select the speed. It's always best to go for a speed which is just a little bit slower than you might first think is suitable. Once you have established a style and tempo look for a button marked `synchrostart'. Once that has been pressed you are ready to go. The automatic chord section on the keyboard is usually clearly marked at the bottom left hand side. Press the required autochord note where it appears above the words you are singing. Initially people can experience some difficulty in keeping time with the keyboard. They are relentless machines and very few of them wait for the singer! They are played best with just one finger in the left hand and be very careful to press only one key at a time.

Here is a little rote which is worth remembering:
- Set the style
- Adjust the tempo
- Press the synchro–start
- Begin your music.

And a few last words
It's very easy to get your mind into an overload situation if accompaniment work is new to you. Practise is very important to make your accompaniment playing almost automatic. Set yourself a long–term goal to write out and learn one song per week. By the end of 20 weeks you will have 20 pieces of card with 20 songs on it, which is a least an hour's worth of material readily available and at your fingertips. You will need to learn the chords for each new song and add them to your vocabulary.

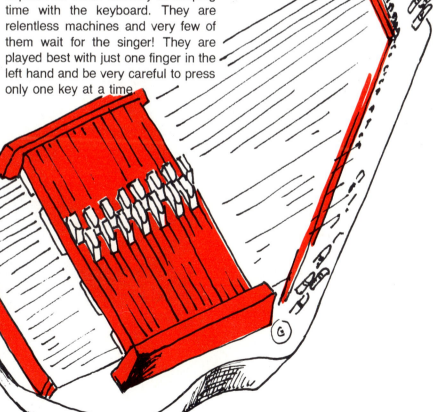

chromaharp

WORD SONG SHEETS (Large Print A4), PO Box 149, NG3 5PU   PLAY THE CHROMAHARP, Kate Baxter, PO Box 149, NG3 5PU
CHROMAHARPS (15 & 21 bar models) from Music Education Supplies Ltd, 101 Banstead Road South, Sutton, Surrey SM2 5LH
61

OUR INSTRUMENTS
Recorded music

Building a library
Music you can listen to and appreciate, invest some sparkle into a warm-up . . . dance . . . play along with or even create an exciting sound track to theatrical activities.

So a good starting point is to build yourself a library. It could be fun looking through your old record collection, but don't worry if you're not a collector, public libraries often lend music and you could always ask friends and colleagues.

Choose carefully, look for variety and contrast, different styles, tempo and 'moods'.

Here are a few ideas.

Electronic music
A rich source of sound with creative and re-creative potential. Its varied moods can make it very suitable for relaxing movement and it is a powerful medium for dance drama.

Authentic musics from around the world
You will find these only on cassette. The non-melodic stimulating rhythms of African drumming are very evocative. Simple activities like walking in lines, diagonals and creating wheels, are most effective and can lead to more intricate floor patterning.

Circle dancing is a universal 'language' without speech; it can involve all ages and cultures in a unifying and spiritual experience.

A mosaic of dance
★Make a cassette of short pieces of music that have lots of contrast. Because the music is different, so will the dance be.

★"What does the music make you think of, Marion? Would you like to come into the circle and dance?" says the leader. Marion starts and the leader sometimes joins her, supporting and enlarging her movements. (North American Indians traditionally danced with a shawl. It can help to focus on a visual and tactile object).

Remember
●the over-use of recorded music, particularly for a captive audience, can be intrusive and a personal irritant.

●using one's own voice and selected instruments, however humble these efforts may be, are so often more satisfying than playing a cassette of someone else's music.

Make a Video
Meeting your own specific needs by venturing into video-making is very satisfying. This is a powerful learning aid.

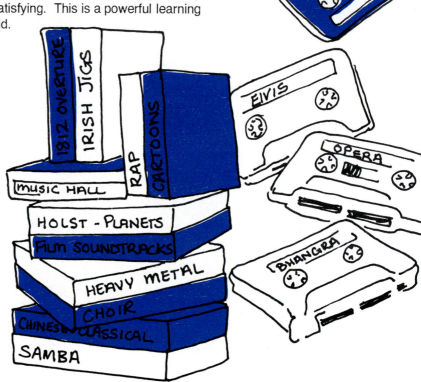

COMMUNICATE WITH VIDEO, Video and Booklet, John Bowkett, 252 Musters Road, West Bridgford, Nottingham NG2 7DR

CODA
Thoughts and Observations

Communication through touch

This very important aspect of getting through to people is in danger of being diminished because of a present day dilemma.

Touch is vital for being reassured of love, approval and acclaim. Throughout life we all need this. It is particularly important to those living in institutionalized settings and the visually and hearing impaired: touch in many instances is the only way of making contact.

Music can be conducted through touch, rather than visual control, and it is often more reassuring. A time for simple massage built into a session is a relaxing wind-down and confirms that touch need not be punitive or provocative.

The hearing-impaired should not be excluded from musical experience. Basic communication can be enhanced through the use of sign language or Makaton for conveying basic information.

Sign languages exist all over the world for deaf people. In Britain over 50,000 use BSL (British Sign Language). It is a specific visual-gesture language that includes expressive use of eyes, face and body to convey meaning.

TOUCH and COMMUNICATION, Christopher Knill, LDA, Wisbech, Cambridgeshire

SIGNS MAKE SENSE, Cath Smith, Souvenir Press

CODA
Thoughts and Observations

Motor and rhythmic development

Coordination problems tend to get thrown together in one very large box. Here is a spotlight on two of them. Because the suggestions need talking about and trying out, do work with a friend.

Q:Why is skipping difficult for so many children?
Q:Why are some children unable to tap a word–pattern?

The answers to both question is about physical and rhythmic development.
Being told you're "not playing or moving in time" is sometimes because of a physical and not a rhythmic difficulty!

On your own, experiment using right R and left L hands. If a tuned instrument is not available just use your hands and shadow play. Try it with your feet too.

G G D G

R R L R

G D G D

R L R L

Which is easier? The second one is likely to be, because there is a physical difficulty of `repetition on one side' in the first example. This is a development from playing `alternate' sides as in the second example.

A:Skipping requires foot repetition on one side and a long short/long short pattern, both fairly complex.
A:Playing pattern (e.g. all syllables of words) is a development from playing just the pulse.

The main steps outlined below are intended only as a rough guide:

Motor Development

Both hands together establishes wholeness of self. It is our earliest gross motor activity. Centering hands in midline usually follows.

Separate hands moving on alternate sides establishes our two–sidedness. Linked with development from crawling to walking.

Separate hands with a repetition on one side. The strong hand begins to emerge here.

Crossing midline. Moving one hand across the centre of the body. This involves crossing the integrating area that joins left and right brain.

Double crossing mid line. Moving both hands simultaneously across the body. This skill is needed for the Charleston – a dance many find difficult for that reason.

The above outline also applies to feet.

In dance, the coordination of hands and feet comes from a feeling pulse within the centre of our body, not a thinking pulse in our heads.

Rhythmic development

Within each of us coexist metric rhythm (heart beat) and free rhythm (breath flows and speech). Awareness of rhythm starts in the womb and the sucking action is our first pulse response. Being moved, bounced up and down, rocked and sung to increases awareness of pulse through physical sensation. Pattern emerges from our heart beat, and grows from different combinations of strong and weak stresses

Hello

Feeling Tired

Goodbye

I love you

Pattern in music increases in

complexity using triplets

dotted rhythms

and syncopation

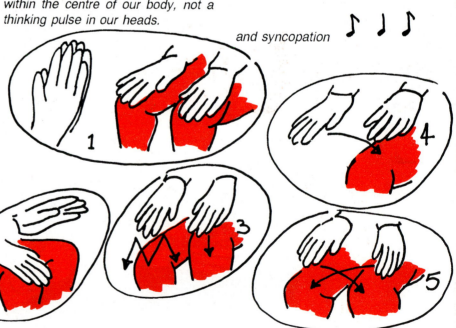

SCOOBERLY–DOOBERLY–DIDDLY–DI–DO, Cassette & Booklet, John Childs, 167 Big Barn Lane, Mansfield, Notts NG18 3LN and LOQOMOCION (songs to promote fine and gross motor movement)

CODA
Thoughts and Observations

Whole body experience

Very young children will mostly play tuned instruments in a 'free' way, gradually developing a feeling for pulse and then pattern [VN3.12]. This pre-verbal stage links with scribble language where the fun and enjoyment of listening and exploring are the priorities. As the motor skills develop, so must the rhythmic interaction between music and movement be fostered for a whole-body experience. To interpret composed music in movement, to improvise simple sequences – to develop fantasy and feeling they need to function together.

Evaluation

Here are ten clips from the video which relate to the development of motor and rhythmic skills as outlined in this section.

A group evaluation could be helpful here. A staff session, perhaps?

VN1:2
Andrew uses both hands together and a basic pattern response.

VN3:15
Tuned instruments require the skill of 'sticking', ie using beaters with two hands to achieve balanced and rhythmic playing. Note the syncopated pattern on the xylophone and the conker beaters!

VN1:6 & 7
Both hands in function grasp on the Lycra balance the body for a pulse response in movement.

VN1:15
The fair child in pale blue has progressed to alternate hands.

VN1:16
Bobby and Clare both use basic rhythmic and motor skills ie pulse and both hands together.

VN1:26
Mixing pulses of two and three and singing in dotted rhythm and crossing midline; shows challenges well met!

VN3:9
Sarah feels secure enough physically and rhythmically to adjust her pulse accompaniment to the speed of the singers.

VN1:11
Lauren in the red Lycra is given a whole body movement experience. The vocal accompaniment of high and low sounds increases her enjoyment. She is moved to laughter!

VN3:13
Maureen uses a finger plectrum to play a pulse-stroke accompaniment on the chromaharp. Watch when she develops into pattern at "all through the day"

VN1:27
Problems of laterality and crossing midline are apparent. Individual confusion of handedness arises from non-acceptance of left-handedness in Romania.

GUIDELINES TO TEACHING DALCROZE EURYTHMICS, Elizabeth Vanderspa, Barton Cottage, Stowford, Lewdown, Devon EX20 4BZ

CODA
Thoughts and Observations

The creative spark

The first stages of being captivated by what we hear and see have impact. We are drawn in, become involved. We are moved – an emotional state has begun. Maria Montessori observed the development of this 'beginning' into activity of immense absorption. She described it as a "ray of concentration where the child is oblivious to the outside world". Her observations were with special needs children in Italy in 1912. Her comments were that watching and giving feedback on what happened and why were more helpful than intervention. How can we achieve this 'lighting up' of the creative spark in our everyday work? So often it will spring from impulse work, or picking upon an unexpected contribution, going down an unplanned pathway. Making a newness, for everyone to react to.

Rosemarie (4 years) cried when she saw the alto xylophone had lost some of its bars. "Have they gone to hospital?" she asked.

Can setting up a Pentatonic scale too early stop exciting music happening? Plays, stories, hop-scotch and exploration games?

Does leaving all the notes on prove too confusing? If we don't, then how does the child who can pick out a tune do so?

If Johnnie sets up a random scale (a disarrangement of the normal scale) does this delay his recognition and learning?

Benedict (9 years) had explored a lot of the sound makers from the old basket. Which one was he going to choose and play? He chose seven – and silently began to build them, some on top of each other, balancing carefully, light on heavy, until it was finished. He stood back with a look of real satisfaction on his face. He called it his 'music machine'. He played it for us with incredible delicacy of movement so that it didn't fall down. It was a breathtaking performance. Applause.

Next day he said "I dreamt about my music machine".

Look again at the physical structure the boys built with their sound-makers from the environment [VN2.1]. It had a shape. They were aware of the tactile and optical possibilities, as well as the acoustic ones.

Looking at instruments in this way opens up a maze of ideas. Sometimes a question like "Which is the shortest bar?" or "Is this a warm or a cold instrument?" will press a new starter.

A final thought from a team who worked in Romania.

"We will share our skills so that you can show your music, drama and dreams to us, and others".

66

FINALE

This may be the end of the book, but we hope that it is, for you, the beginning or further development of your work with *Fundamental Activities*. These materials come from a variety of sources and situations and are not restricted in their use to any one culture or context.

Many of them were given a new focus from being explored with children, parents, teachers and carers in Romania. It was in many ways a harsh environment for the seeds of these ideas to be planted. But they were enthusiastically and carefully nurtured and we think they will grow and develop rich fruit.

We hope that the ideas and activities will open up new possibilities for you in the education of children and adults, whether you are already experienced or just starting out. If *Fundamental Activities* does succeed in providing this kind of help and stimulus, it will certainly have justified the many thousands of hours of work which have gone into its production.

CONTRIBUTORS

Grateful thanks to all these generous people who gave their thoughts, time and text to the Handbook.

Heidi Arndt	Primary School Teacher
Duncan Chapman	Community Musician
John Childs	Regional Arts Coordinator, Nottinghamshire
Tim Gauntley	Canadian Educator and Chromaharpist
Ann Griffin	Headteacher Primary School
Susan Hughes	Special Needs Teacher
Barbara Jones	Freelance Consultant in Special Needs
Isabel Jones	Voice and movement specialist
Olga Lake	Musician and dancer working with elderly
Sheila Perkins	Mother, Counsellor and Nursery Teacher
Wendy Prevezer	Speech and language therapist using music for communication
Margaret Ralph	General Inspector of Education, London Borough of Bromley
Beth Salmon	Secondary School Teacher, Dance and Drama Specialist
Peter Sidaway	Freelance Consultant in Music Education
Lizzie Spring	Aromatherapist and writer
Ivan Stott	Music and Theatre Animateur
Mary Turner	Community Artist